The
ELEPHANT'S TALE

The
ELEPHANT'S TALE

LONDON TO VLADIVOSTOK ON TWO WHEELS

MIKE HANNAN

NEW
HOLLAND

First published in 2012 by New Holland Publishers
London • Sydney • Cape Town • Auckland

86 Edgware Road London W2 2EA United Kingdom
1/66 Gibbes Street Chatswood NSW 2067 Australia
Wembly Square First Floor Solan Street Gardens Cape Town 8000 South Africa
218 Lake Road Northcote Auckland New Zealand

www.newhollandpublishers.com
www.newholland.com.au

A record of this book is held at the National Library of Australia

ISBN 9781742572512

Publisher: Patsy Rowe
Publishing Manager: Lliane Clarke
Project Editor: Anthony Nott
Designer: Kim Pearce
Photographs: Jo Hannan
Production Manager: Olga Dementiev
Printer: Toppan Leefung Printing Ltd (China)

10 9 8 7 6 5 4 3 2 1

Keep up with New Holland Publishers on Facebook and Twitter www.facebook.com/
NewHollandPublishers

Twitter: @NewHollandpub
and: @NewHollandAU

To my wife Jo, who is the heart of Team Elephant

He who would travel happily must travel light.
– Antoine de Saint-Exupéry

Contents

The Elephant's Journey

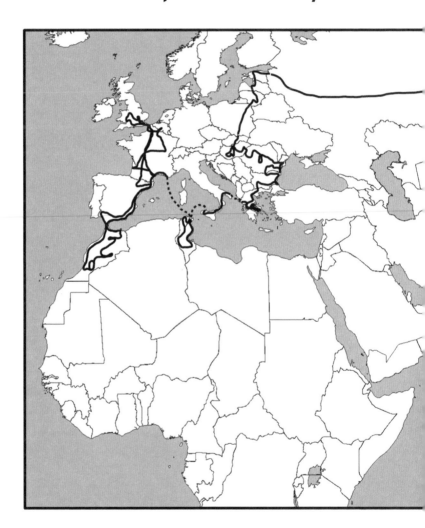

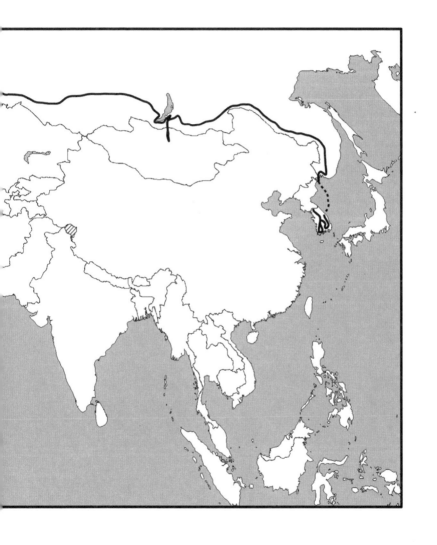

1

Small Beginnings

This is the story of a journey, of two baby-boomers afraid to grow old and of the motorbike they came to call Elephant. It begins with both uncertainty and possibility, as many journeys do, and ends with new uncertainty and new possibility, as journeys often do. They say that every journey begins with a single step. If this is so, then the first step on this journey was imperceptibly small. A tiny shift in mind set, a distracted feeling at work and, somewhere, a growing feeling that life was short and precious and there to be lived. These were the small beginnings of this journey.

We had seen the same disquiet in other baby-boomers. It is the restlessness that fuels an economy of grey nomads and drives a fleet of cruise ships and convoys of packaged adventure travellers. It is as though a generation, brought up on the myth of its own youthful energy, was refusing to sit down and be quiet as their parents and grandparents had done. I remember some years before when our daughter Sarah, who had left home and started working for law firm, had jokingly complained that she would have to work forever to pay tax for the huge numbers of baby-boomers about to retire. This brought a sharp response from a wounded father. What she didn't seem to understand, I said, was that the boomers had changed every phase of life as they had passed through it and they would change retiring and dying as well. If she wanted to be rich, I blustered, she should give up law and get into adventure tourism for geriatrics! It seems that every generation has its own hubris to be foisted on the next.

During the first 20 years of our marriage, my wife Jo and I had lived the nomadic life of a military family, raising our children all over the world. For the next ten, we settled in Canberra, the Australian capital, while our two children slugged their way through college and university. Jo worked as a high school science teacher through our Canberra years. She was lucky enough to work in the same school throughout this time (the school attended by both our offspring) and enjoyed the opportunity to establish her own career and circle of friends after a stop-start working life following the flag. For my part, I prospered as a bureaucrat inside the Department of Defence and as a manager in civil industry.

Our Canberra years gave us a time of stability that allowed Sarah and our son Nick to take advantage of their educational opportunities and for the four of us to enjoy the excellent facilities of this small city. Despite these advantages, I never really took to the place. The cool winters gave my arthritic joints a beating and each spring brought on three months of hay fever misery. I might have put up with these disadvantages, but in the end, I found the city's relentlessly well-ordered demeanour stifling. Ten years was enough.

By the year 2006, with both our children grown and educated, Jo and I had sold up in Canberra to move to the Gold Coast where I had the offer of a good job in manufacturing. Regardless of the reason for selection, however, the Gold Coast proved an interesting antidote to the slumberous capital. This was one of those decision points in life that everyone comes to from time to time. We had an opportunity to remake our life and started to imagine other possibilities for our future. We had been frugal and had some investments set up for retirement. We had our good health. In short, we had options.

But having options and making a change is not the same thing. We started to talk about possible futures, to consider how we might change and what we might do. Our first discussions were philosophical enough but still led to some early decisions. We made the necessary pact not to go quietly into the next part of our lives; we took up dancing, and Jo learnt to scuba dive. We also reinvigorated our interest in motorbikes and were soon regularly riding in the hills of the Gold Coast hinterland.

Jo and I have always loved motorbikes and if we were not as bike-active in our child-rearing years as we would have liked, the passion remained strong. We have always had at least one bike in the shed (often two or three), and harboured the belief that we would get back into the saddle one day. Within a short time of arriving on the Coast we had joined three suitably conservative motorbike clubs and started to enjoy some longer distance rides exploring the country within striking distance of the Gold Coast. Our road bike at the time was a Kawasaki GTR 1000, an old design but still fast and bullet-proof.

All of this was good fun but we were still unsettled. Looking back now I see that deep inside there remained the last embers of an almost forgotten dream; one of those dreams you don't ever talk about. A selfish dream. A dream put aside for career and family; a dormant, dusty, shadowy dream. You see, in my fanciful youth I had wanted to ride a motorbike around the world. It was a dream I had willingly put aside for career, marriage and family, but a dream that had never been fully extinguished.

Our offspring, as they often are, were well ahead of us. As a family we had enjoyed following the Brumbies (the capital's champion rugby team) and the Wallabies (the national team). After enjoying the Rugby World Cup, which was played in Australia in 2003, we had made a family pact to travel to France for the Rugby World Cup in 2007. This would not be much of a stretch for our daughter who had moved to London with her partner in 2005. To provide some extra incentive for the trip, Sarah was planning to marry in the UK immediately following the World Cup final. I would like to think that this bit of considerate timing was the result of an excellent upbringing, but as her partner is a keen England supporter, I suspect there were other forces at work.

As the World Cup games were spread all over France, with one game to be played by the Wallabies in Wales, we started to plan based on the need to travel between the venues. It didn't take long before we were considering travel by motorbike and were investigating the options for buying and selling, renting, or shipping our own bike over and back. When we raised the idea of shipping the bike to Europe and riding around on our Rugby adventure, the kids responded by giving us a copy of Chris Scott's *Adventure Motorcycling Handbook* and John Hermann's *motorbike Journeys through the Alps and Corsica*! From there it was all downhill. We devoured the books and our imaginations started to race. If we were going for a few months, why not longer? If we did stay on, what about the winter? There were a dozen other questions like these and we wallowed in the forming detail of our emerging plan. Talking about it and actually doing it, however, are still not the same. The sad fact is that we may never have moved beyond exotic talk if not for the unfortunate death of our friend Maureen Waters.

Maureen was a fellow Ulysses Club member, regular ride companion, friend, and general good bloke. She was determined and single minded. She knew what she wanted and put some people off-side because of this. She had a lovely Suzuki SV 650S and rode it hard. Having come to bikes later in life than many of us, she probably rode it too hard. One Sunday, on her way back from a motorbike rally at Tamworth, she slammed into a car and was killed. After the initial shock and our anger at her having done such a thing had dissipated a little, we realised some truths about Maureen's death that helped us to reconcile the loss. Maureen had been lucky in many ways. She had often said to her fellow riders that we were the most important people in her life and that riding was what she wanted to do most. She had lived life on her own terms and died doing what she loved. Most of us don't get that chance. The lesson for us was obvious and we didn't need a counsellor to point it out. If I truly had a dream, then I needed to spell it out to see if Jo could buy into it and then get on with it and live it. It needed to move from feel-good talk to hard miles on the road. So we started to talk. Consensus emerged (the lady has always been a sucker for an adventure) and soon there was the outline of a plan.

We were pleased that we were able to reach a decision but were left wondering about how many other dreams we had abandoned, or simply not allowed to flourish, for lack of the will to make the decision. Some of this is easily reconcilable. Where one of us had dreams that were not shared by the other, compromises were made and deals done. That's the way relationships work. But others were stillborn or abandoned. Perhaps they were just too personal or too risky to even talk about.

Typically, there were many strong reasons to decide not to go on a motorbike journey. We both had ageing parents, neither of us had our youthful energy and strength any more and we were not so financially secure that we could make this journey without considerable financial pain. But in the end we decided that there would always be a dozen reasons not to do this or many other things in our life. Finding an excuse not to do something is always the simple option. This time we decided not to take it.

As we talked the days marched by, but by the middle of May 2007 we had made the important decisions. We would ship our bike to Europe for the Rugby World Cup and keep going. We would try our best to ride to Vladivostok and the end of continental Europe. Succeed or fail we would keep the faith.

The obvious question at this point is: why ride a bike anyway? Lots of folk have perfectly satisfactory journeys without the problem of caring for and riding a bike. Others who undertake long distance motorbike travel have said that the only folk who ask why anyone would undertake such a journey are those who don't understand the answer when they hear it. I'm not sure about this, but I do know that there are those who *get* bikes and those who don't. Those who don't are usually the folk who ask, 'what's it worth?'. When you tell them the retail price, they respond, 'you could buy a good car for that', as though a motorbike could only be a cheap alternative to a car. Those who *get* bikes love the way they work and the relationship between the bike and the rider. They love the way bikes make you feel; the sheer exhilaration of it. Besides, as we were about to find out, riding a bike can teach you some useful lessons about life, if you care to learn them.

Making the decision to try and ride our bike more than halfway around the world was hard work and, having gotten that bit of unpleasantness out of the way, we settled back to await the start of our adventure. A couple of weeks of reverie drifted by before the obvious became obvious: nothing would happen because we wished it, we needed to do some work! We had heard it said that you need to spend as long planning a trip like this as you intend to spend on it. One year on the road meant one year in planning. We had only weeks to get ready and we were not even sure where we wanted to go. We needed at least a general itinerary to give us a framework for planning but even this seemed designed to frustrate us. To start with, the Rugby World Cup and our daughter's wedding were timed to leave us in northern Europe at the start of winter. This didn't seem like a good beginning to us. At the same time we needed to assemble the gear we would take, starting with the motorbike. Our ageing Kawasaki had served us well but was not the bike for this trip. Reluctantly we put it up for sale and replaced it with a near new 2006 BMW GS Adventure, a purpose built adventure motorbike.

The new bike was fitted with high quality Hepco and Becker luggage and looked the part for the type of travel we had in mind. Mind you, our relationship with the Beemer was slow to warm at best. Compared with the Kawasaki it replaced, it was rough running, down on revs and power, uncomfortable and downright difficult to manoeuvre at slow speed. Some changes were needed! Top priority was a new seat. If we were to sit on this thing most days for a year, then something better than the picket fence that came with the bike was needed. We had a local expert make up a new seat which we trialled on a seven hour ride around the forestry tracks of northern NSW. First problem sorted.

Storage was at a premium on the Beemer so some quick action to provide some extra hidey-holes was needed. A small dashboard was fashioned from stainless steel and mounted on the bars to take the GPS, phone and sunnies. The bead breaker and tyre levers were stowed in a PVC tube behind the left side box and a larger diameter tube behind the right box provided quick access to puncture repair tools and a tent fly. A rush job over three weekends fashioned a hard tank bag from fibreglass that would lock onto the tank using a special bracket screwed to the filler collar. Despite the mad dash to get it finished, it was not ready before the bike shipped. Still, enough was done to confirm that we could have a secure, waterproof tank bag and we would just have to take the finished box with us and marry it up later.

As part of the tank project, we purchased a pair of cycling bags normally used pannier-style over the front wheels of a bicycle. By changing the fittings and organising a harness system on the Beemer, these sat neatly on either side of the fuel tank. The thinking was that these small bags would be our daypacks that we could easily disconnect from the bike and carry with us with a shoulder strap. This had never been possible with traditional tank bags.

A final trip to the auto electrician to get the intercom, GPS and phone connections hard-wired and to get some extra power points front and rear, and all that could be done in the time was done. A weekend spent building a crate from scrap steel and covering it with plastic core-flute preceded a couple of frantic nights cutting it up and remaking it 150 mm shorter. Fortunately I remembered at the last minute that the bike needed to go sideways into a standard container and took the trouble to roll out the tape measure! There was still one last night of crating, packing and strapping. Our riding suits, suit liners, long underwear, neck warmers, tool kits and spare parts were all jammed into the panniers and locked down. The bike was strapped down on the pallet and the sides screwed in place. It was ready. On a Thursday morning in late May I drove the crate to Brisbane and dropped it off at the shipping agent and it was done. We stood staring at the empty garage that afternoon and for the first time we knew that we were really going.

We also knew that once we stopped work our life would be all expense and no income so a lot of time was spent developing and refining a budget. First, we carefully charted our household budget and identified what would need to be paid as an ongoing expense while we were away. These items became the first outgoings on our travel budget. We then filled out the remainder of the budget using some broad (or gaping) assumptions about costs. We wanted the budget to be robust enough so that we wouldn't have to rework it every time we changed plans. The process eventually gave us our total spend for the year, the timing and amount of the major expenses both domestic and travel, and a rough daily allowance to cover accommodation, food, fuel and entertainment.

By this stage, with about a month before we were due to depart, we settled on a broad itinerary. First we would pick up the bike in London, follow the Rugby World Cup around France and Wales, and attend our daughter's wedding near Oxford, England. That was the easy part. All of the games had fixed dates and locations. Next, with the late October weather starting to chill, we would head to Spain. When the weather became too cold there, we planned to cross over to Morocco for the first part of the winter. We would then find a way along the coast from Morocco to Tunisia and Libya. After surviving the worst of the winter, we would cross back to Europe through Greece and ride north to cross into Russia around the top of Belarus before heading east with side trips to Kazakhstan and Mongolia. We planned to be in Vladivostok in early August 2008 and to ship the bike home from there.

Using the net, we booked some flights, enough to get us going, and some accommodation, enough to get us started. Our budget was already starting to creak and D-Day was still weeks away. A visit to the travel doctor was another round of financial misery. Fortunately we were given blood tests to determine our level of anti-bodies for the common diseases. After years of travelling to 'interesting' places, we had been inoculated so many times that we had immunity to Every Disease Known to Man (EDKM), or at least the common strains, so we were spared the worst of the misery. Nonetheless, two rounds of injections and funny tasting liquids left us out of pocket by hundreds of Australian dollars. And that was just the beginning. Being of mature disposition, we both had to acquire enough drugs of various sorts to last a year or so (more money) along with a range of medical supplies sufficient for a small war.

But it wasn't finished. Dental checks, spare glasses, updated wills, overseas medical insurances, mail redirection, travelling clothes, GPS mapping and all sorts of other 'special' purchases clocked up day by day. Not much of this was included in the budget, which, conveniently, started on departure day, and we were already eating into money put aside for travel. While we watched the money flow out, there was plenty to keep our minds occupied. Dozens of documents needed to be copied or scanned into the computer. Our contact files were brought up to date, newspaper deliveries were stopped and all manner of services and insurances were suspended. There were several meetings with the accountant and financial adviser during which we tried to convince ourselves that we could do this and not sentence ourselves to a life of penury. We developed a feeling that the adventure would not be pain free in the years to come but we put it out of our minds and pressed on. Sometimes you just have to do that.

When we started to eat out the larder and give away the meat from our freezer to neighbours, we knew we were close. Emptying our swimming pool and making cotton drops to cover the doors and windows was another clue. But what sealed the thing was the morning, with just a day to go, that we pumped out our waterbed and moved into the guest room. Now this might seem like a small thing in the scheme of things, but we had been very happy in that bed for nearly 20 years. It had always been a comfort and a sanctuary. Cosy and comfortable on a cold night and always welcoming after the shortest trip away, this was *our* personal space. Now it was gone. Our life had been simplified and disentangled from our world to the point that we were camping in our own home. It was time to go.

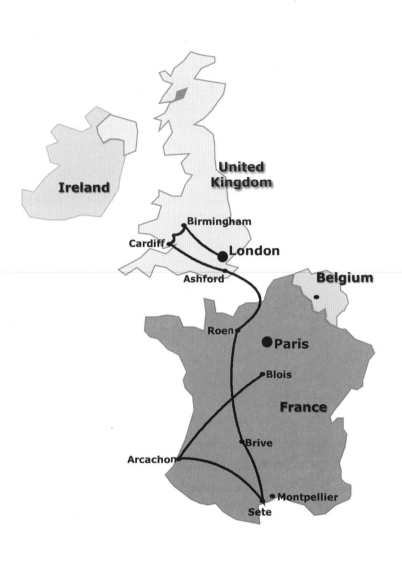

Ireland

United
Kingdom

Birmingham

Cardiff

London

Ashford

Belgium

Roen

Paris

Blois

France

Brive

Arcachon

Montpellier

Sete

2

Learning the Ropes

On 27 August 2007 we flopped into a Qantas jet heading east sure that we had left the stove on, or failed to lock the back door. We didn't care. We were away. First stop New York.

New York got onto the itinerary because it was the best route to Europe that allowed me to use some frequent flyer points and, since we were passing, we decided to stop and have a few days to see the city. Having not given any particular thought to our visit, we arrived without any preconceptions and loved the place from the jump. This was our kind of village! It was big, rambunctious, smelly, crowded, cosmopolitan, decaying and exciting. Everything good, bad and indifferent is in New York.

Going via New York allowed us to do some important shopping as well as the essential sight-seeing. Jo and I both found down parkas at a good price as well as a small mountaineering stove and fuel bottle. Jo also bought new walking shoes and I found a good light-weight, micro-fibre shirt. It was our first hunting and gathering expedition on this journey and we were pleased to escape with our wallets and our sense of humour intact.

The escape to London, however, was not without its drama. The cheapest flight we could find was with Aer Lingus which staged through Dublin, a smallish hub run with such incompetence that it gave the impression of a great hub on a bad day. We missed our connection into London milling about with the crowd and could easily have missed the second flight. Not for the last time we noticed that the current obsession with airport security created a level of chaos that was a significant security problem in its own right.

Our daughter Sarah and her partner Mike had a small one-bedroom apartment close to the centre of London near St Paul's. They had very generously taken some leave and gone to France for a week to lessen the congestion in the shoe box, leaving us with a perfect base for the last of our administration. Jo used to live in London and I had been there often enough not to feel the need to do any tourist stuff. Instead we walked a lot, both to improve our fitness and because there was a tube strike, and got on with sorting the last of the administration for our journey.

Insurance was the biggest problem and it took several days of effort to find a company prepared to insure our foreign registered bike. When we found one, the price was enough to make the eyes water. Still, it was necessary and, in the end, done. Our policy covered the bike for compulsory 3rd party and comprehensive insurance anywhere in the EU, but would lapse after the bike had been out of the UK for three months. We knew that this could prove to be a problem later in the trip but it was the best option available.

The first of the Wallabies' Rugby World Cup pool matches was scheduled for Saturday 8 September in Lyon, France and the next was one week later in Cardiff, Wales. Game three was back to southern France to Montpellier. We studied our newly purchased UK and France maps closely and decided that if we rode the bike from the pick up in London to Lyon, then back to Cardiff and back across the Channel to Montpellier we would just flog ourselves for no useful purpose. It wasn't too much of a wrench, therefore, for us to leave the bike in its crate at the depot for another few days and to organise a flying visit to Lyon for game one. Lufthansa flew us to Lyon via Munich the Friday before the game and we then took the 'scenic' suburban bus into town to find our hotel in the older part of town.

Our daughter Sarah and her partner Mike were still in France in the Champagne district. They hurried off to Paris on the Friday afternoon to meet our son Nick, who flew in via Vietnam, then drove down to Lyon to meet us. It was the first time the family had been together for more than a year with Sarah in London, Nick in Canberra and us on the Gold Coast. It was also the fulfilment of our little pact made four years before, during the 2003 Rugby World Cup.

Lyon was built slightly up stream from the confluence of the Rhône and the Saône where its Roman founders could defend the crossings over these two substantial rivers. Fortifications were built on the high ground on the western bank of the Saône and a thriving city grew up along the thin isthmus between the converging flows. Like many modernised European cities, Lyon's old historic heart was well restored and had a distinct touristy feel to it. We found that the old Roman ruins were unremarkable with a little too much 1960s' concrete around for our taste. But, the inevitable Notre Dame Cathedral, which took pride of place on the high ground and offered stunning views over the rivers and the rolling plains to the east, was well worth the climb. Of most interest to us, however, were the remnants of the town's central role in developing a French silk industry at a time when silk was the preserve of the Chinese. The old silk workshops were long gone, the buildings converted into densely packed residentials held together with a maze of tiny lanes and private courtyards. It was, nonetheless, easy to imagine the crush and bustle of the place when the spinning workshops were at their peak.

Outside of the historic centre, the town looked liveable and comfortable, but we quickly discovered that the French were poorly organised for the RWC crowds. Transport to the stadium by train was chaotic and crowd control so slapdash that only the good humour of the public stopped it all turning sour. Still, the Wallabies had an easy win over Japan and we celebrated the success of our RWC pact at a two star restaurant called *Le Bec* which was a short walk from our hotel. The French don't give their stars easily and the food was excellent. The degustation menu seemed like a good idea when we were ordering it, but we ate far too much and I didn't sleep well curled up around an overstuffed belly.

It was dark in London by the time we got back to the flat to drop off the last of our non-bike clothing and repack for bike riding. We then lugged our gear to the tube station and rode out to the suburb of Wembley and an old hotel close to the pick-up depot for the bike.

As soon as business was open on Monday morning we were off to a nearby suburb to buy a new battery for the bike. Although the battery on the bike should have had plenty of life in it, we knew it would be flat after shipping and we didn't want to take a chance on it for the remainder of the 12-month journey. With the advantage of hindsight, we should have jump-started the battery we had and saved the money. As we would discover, there were lots of harder problems to solve in remote places than a flat battery.

Picking up the bike the next day was easy. The depot staff helped us unpack and then reassemble the bike then we changed the battery, got the engine started, and we were off. We left the steel crate with the depot staff who had offered to break it up and dispose of it for us.

Back at the pub we finally had the bike and our gear in the same place and could start packing. Because the bike had left before we had assembled all of our equipment or completed the new tank box, we didn't know if it would all fit. We spent a long evening carefully folding and packing, then repacking, then culling, then repacking again. We cursed our lack of preparations for the trip but consoled each other with the reality that had we done *all* of the essential preparation, we would still be in Queensland.

The next morning we loaded the luggage onto the bike and stood back to look at our handy work. Somehow it was fitted, and it looked reasonably neat and tidy. The new tank box had needed some modification but seemed secure and didn't look too agricultural, and the two-tank sidebags were neat enough. It only remained to be seen how well it handled the rigours of life on the road.

More concerning to me was the size and weight of the beast. The BMW had always been a big, tall bike, but with the full load, rider and pillion, it was big, tall and heavy. For the first time I had some real misgivings about my own ability to ride it where we wanted to go, and of the bike's ability to withstand the beating it was sure to get. I kept my own counsel on this as Jo and I stood back and looked at the full rig for the first time. This was our world now. If it wasn't on the bike, it was no longer something we really needed. From here on our lives would become much simpler, and much more complicated.

Now that we were reunited with the bike, we started to have some confidence in our plan. From London we would ride to

Wales for the game in Cardiff then turn south to tour the south coast as far as Portsmouth where we would get a ferry to France before riding down to Montpellier for the third pool game. We would then meander over to Bordeaux for game four. After that, it all got a little fuzzy again but, as we were discovering, you don't need the best plan, just a plan.

Like all good bikers, I had no choice but to detour on our trip to Wales to visit the National Motorcycle Museum at Solihull near Birmingham! We rationalised that the short run from London would settle down the bike and calm some of my nerves at the prospect of a year with this monster motorbike. A couple of hours easy cruise up the motorway would see us looking over the exhibits and thinking about a cold (imported) beer.

As sometimes happens, what seemed the simplest part proved the hardest. In our first hour out of London we covered only 19 miles (30 kilometres). It was a very bad start. We sweltered in our riding suits in the unseasonably hot weather. The clutch started to smell as I struggled to come to grips with the rolling mass in the stop-start traffic and, the icing on the cake, the engine started to run hot. The new sidebags must have been affecting the airflow over the motor more than I had anticipated.

We started out trying to keep the early euphoria of our departure going with some cheerful banter but after the first grim hour we had sunk into a deep silence. We both knew that there was nothing else for it but to hunker down over the controls and get on with it. It was an approach we would use a lot in the months ahead. Early in the second hour we crossed onto the north-bound motorway and picked up cruising speed. The engine temperature came back down to normal and the bike got easier to ride. Happily, as our speed rose we found that the load didn't upset the handling of the bike excessively. The bike also showed a smartish turn of speed in overtaking.

By early afternoon we had found the museum and paid our entrance fee. The National motorbike Museum is dedicated to British bikes and has an amazing collection. There are many unique exhibits often displayed in complete sets showing the development of the most famous models from prototype to end of production. Unfortunately there are so many bikes that there is only space to show the most important machines to full advantage. The remainder are cluttered in cheek by jowl. The interesting aspect for me was the number of prototype models on display. Many showed developments that had been exploited by Japanese and Italian manufacturers while the British industry slid into decline. The ideas and technology that might have allowed the British manufacturers to compete were largely stillborn without proper investment or lost to the ugly workplace culture that paralysed British manufacturing during the 1960s. As well as a remarkable tribute to a once strong and innovative industry, this museum was, for me, also a museum of lost opportunities.

After the National motorbike Museum, we took the economy-class tour of Birmingham. Despite our best efforts to see it at its worst by riding the late night local buses, and our failure to find any real Brum-Balti food, we quite liked the place.

With several days before the Cardiff game we took the scenic route to Abergavenny, at the start of the Brecon Beacons National Park, through a pleasant, cluttered, English countryside. A run over the National Park south-to-north and north-to-south was a suitable introduction to Wales with its bare hills and rain over 300 metres. Interestingly, the National Park was grazed and there were little farming communities all over. Our GPS (which we had, by then, named Kylie) took us via some very small back lanes with lots of blind corners and the surface slick with rain and sheep shit. Despite the conditions, I was starting to feel more comfortable on the bike and getting the hang of the weight at low speeds. By the time we got to the pretty Welsh town of Carmarthen we had had a good ride that left us feeling a little more confident about the journey ahead.

We met up with our son Nick that night, and our daughter Sarah and her partner Mike the next morning. With Sarah and Mike's wedding only a few weeks away, it was also a good chance to meet Mike's dad John who had recently moved to Carmarthen. We all piled into the train for a couple of hours of British Rail entertainment on the way down to Cardiff for game two.

Cardiff was a crush of rugby-mad Welsh supporters by the time we arrived two hours before kick-off. Gold Wallabies strips bobbed along in the flow of the Welsh scarlet slowly rolling towards the stadium from all directions. Any thought we had of a quiet wander around Cardiff City was quickly abandoned and we were carried along with the inexorable flow of the scarlet river to the stadium. We found ourselves at a point opposite to our entry gate so we ambled along with the good-humoured crush, drifting past backwaters of scarlet and gold becalmed around the many pubs and bars. The carnival atmosphere was infectious and, although these two great Rugby playing nations had form going back a hundred years, there was none of the macho, aggressive rub common with some other football codes. The foot soldiers of the scarlet and gold armies stood around amiably enjoying the warm late summer sun and the cool Welsh beer. Mixed patrols scouted the perimeter of the drinking holes; families divided by the colour of their shirts but united by their love of the game they play in heaven and the camaraderie that is central to it.

The Millennium Stadium was magnificent and new. It was definitely the best place we had been to watch rugby. The Amazon flow washing around the perimeter wall of the great building parted into smaller rivers through each entrance gate. We made our way to our gate and moved with the flow higher and higher into the mountainous stands, branching again and again until, in a single file, we were delivered to our seats in the vertigo-inducing alps of the southern end.

The atmosphere was electric and buzzing with anticipation. All around us excited conversations speculated on recent form, recycled opinions and new-found expertise. As the game approached, the crowd settled and the gladiators came out for the national anthems of two warrior nations. Ninety thousand souls stood as one as the Gold supporters let forth with a lusty, full throated rendition of their battle hymn. We felt ourselves swell with pride that our team did not disgrace itself in the singing stakes despite its small numbers. But this was a competition we were never going to win. The Welshmen, of course, knew the words to all the verses of their anthem and knew how to sing. When they stood 80,000 strong and spoke up for their team, the outpouring of deep national spirit washed us away in a flood of emotion and tradition.

The Welsh continued to sing as the game got underway but the singing petered out soon after kick off. It was hard even for the Welsh to stay enthusiastic in their singing while their team was being taken apart. The Gold men from the New World put them to the sword without sentimentality or mercy.

The post-game celebrations didn't seem to suffer from the Welsh loss and disappointment. Perhaps rugby supporters understand that the game they love is so tough that both the victor and the vanquished garner credit from the struggle and deserve a share of the spoils. We let a much quieter river of scarlet carry us down through its tributaries and mighty flows and eventually back to our sleepy village B&B and a quiet continuity that seemed oblivious to the clash of titans that had just taken place a few hours to the south.

Our daughter had booked us smart rural accommodation in one of those quaint 16th Century farm houses that tourists seem to hanker for. It was very picturesque and … well… 'quaint'. I continually hit my head on the low door lintels and the plumbing was at best interesting. We had long since decided that the romance of a traveller's accommodation was only one factor in a happy stay. Here, the romance came with near concussion, ineffective showers in a steamy broom closet and a mind-numbingly expensive tariff. It was at about this point that we started to formulate some views on the type of accommodation we would seek and use for the year ahead. We decided that the three priorities we should always consider were: location in relation to what we wanted to do, price and facilities. We decided that these were the factors that we would balance and that romance would take care of itself. Looking back, it was a good, if inevitable, decision.

Our initial plan was to tour the southern counties and then get a ferry out of Portsmouth to the south of France. This would provide a short and direct route down to Montpellier on the Mediterranean Coast. It also avoided riding back across much of southern England, an area that is densely populated with crowded roads. The plan came unstuck when our insurance company failed to send out our certificate (the so-called Green Card) in time for us to collect it before leaving London. The certificate was essential for travel throughout the EU so there was no option to go without it. There was nothing for it but to return to London and sort it out.

Our run back across the country included a short detour through the Welsh valleys. These original coal mining areas looked much as I remembered them from old movies of D. H. Lawrence novels: bare-arsed hills with bare-arsed towns. The valley towns were a million miles from modern villages like Carmarthen, which are full of cashed up English refugees. We stopped at one pub for a piss-stop and I am sure we were the most interesting thing to happen there that week. If only we could have understood what they were saying I'm sure we would have had a great time with the locals! Still, they were glad to see us on a bleak Sunday and gathered around the bike asking questions about it and our journey. Later we would become used to being a curiosity and skilled at answering questions in languages we didn't understand. On this first occasion, however, we felt like frauds considering the small distance we had travelled on the bike. I did, however, find myself talking about the bike and its rig with a touch of pride for the first time. A few days riding in the wet hills had improved my confidence in its surefootedness. It was still an uneasy relationship and both parties still had something to prove.

Our quick transit of the island led us to Ashford, Kent, located between London and the Channel Tunnel. We hoped this would be a well-located base for some administration. Haircuts were needed and, while this has never been a big deal to me, Jo started an intensive search around the high street looking for a 'suitable' hairdresser. This was a ritual played out many times over the next year and, try as I might, I could never figure out the formula for suitability that might have helped in the search. In the end we both found that short hair was the best option under a helmet and the easiest to keep clean on the road. The only problem with keeping your hair short is that you need to find a hairdresser every couple of weeks.

By the time we had picked up our insurance certificate from London we were short of time to get down to Montpellier for game three. The Channel Tunnel was the quickest option, or so we thought. We arrived at the tunnel in good time for our intended crossing but there was a delay to the service and we spent hours waiting to be called forward to a train. After the call forward, we then sat on the bike in a line for more hours before we were able to board. All of this was only made bearable because it didn't rain. To top off the experience, an emergency alarm was sounded halfway through the tunnel. Vehicles travel through the tunnel on specially constructed multi-deck trains; and when a fuel spill was found in the deck above ours, we were evacuated to the end of the train for the remainder of the trip. This left the bike on its sidestand rocking unattended to the sway of the train with me genuinely worried that it would fall.

We emerged on the French side, riding on the right of the road, four hours later than we had planned and determined to come back by another route. Still, it was good to be out of the UK with its crowded roads and extraordinarily high prices. Two hours on the excellent French motorway south to Rouen cleared the cobwebs and a hearty French dinner put all right with our world again.

We still had a long haul down through central France if we were to be sorted for the game in two days' time. It is at just these vulnerable times that things go wrong. A little miscalculation in the navigation saw our 630-kilometre day extended over 12 hours.

We had decided that we would have a better ride if we stuck to the secondary roads and stayed off the motorways. This was a mistake for a team in a hurry. The villages were clogged with Friday market goers and traffic was often at walking pace. To make matters worse, Kylie took us through some obscure minor roads that added time and stress to the journey. After wasting time like this for most of the day we gave up and headed for the motorway. This became the first test for our rig at high speed and we had some misgivings about its stability. The manufacturer recommended a top speed of 140km/h with the full luggage-fit and since the freeway speed was 130, we thought this would be fine. And it would have been, except that no one drove at the speed limit. We joined the flow and I gradually increased our speed as confidence in the stability of the rig grew. Soon enough we were belting along with the crowd in the not-so-fast-lane while the fast cars and Honda ST1300s blasted past us in the proper fast lane. We were still making very good time. It was 250 kilometres to the overnight stop in Brive. 250 divided by 140 equals… a quick trip to town!

Our son Nick was travelling in a hire car and had gone straight from the Wales game to the south of France. This had given him time to discover that Montpellier would not be the best place to stay for a Rugby World Cup match. Accommodation prices had gone through the roof and the place was full of gold-clad Rugby fans! The town of Sète, an hour to the west of Montpellier on the train, was selected, and proved to be a great little town and an excellent base for the game. The run down from Brive, with a lazy long-lunch, and a wander through interesting back lanes, highways and mountain villages, was just the kind of day we like on a bike. By the time we found Nick at a cheap hotel and turned up a cold beer and some food, our miserable run to Brive was long forgotten.

Sète is a working fishing port, container port and tourist centre. The old town is built on the mainland and two islands formed by a couple of wide, straight, grand canals. There were lots of small cheap eateries and bars tucked in around the central district. Sitting outdoors drinking coffee, in the fading autumn sunshine with the shade-trees turning gold in the first of the cool weather, was deliciously French. We climbed the high hill overlooking the town and were rewarded with a glorious view over the village and the port, and the open sea beyond.

Nick had arrived in town a day before us and had found a cheap hotel right in the centre with a garage for the bike and his little hire car. He had explained in his fractured French that we needed parking for a small car and a moto. Madame assumed 'moto' meant the type of little scooter they ride around there and not the monster we arrived on, which consumed the space normally allocated to a second car. She looked, we shrugged, and we all laughed.

On game day (22 September) the train to Montpellier took about 40 minutes. Montpellier is a university town. It is spacious, easy to get around and was full of uni students returning from the summer break. The old hands were smoking and drinking coffee in the cafés while the freshmen were standing on corners with large suitcases and maps, looking bewildered. University towns have a common feel everywhere. They seem to have a youthful enthusiasm that reflects itself in the public spaces, the cafés and the pace of life. In this aspect at least, Montpellier felt comfortable and familiar and we were lulled into a sense of well-being and Gallic bonhomie.

Now that kick-off was imminent, the reality of French life started to seep through to us. The tramway was the main transport to the stadium but the schedule didn't include any additional services on game day and the huge throng had to make do with a few extra carriages on the standard trains. Jo summed it up best as we spilled out onto the roadway, still a half a kilometre from the stadium, with the words, 'That trip would have been pleasant if I could have breathed.' The crush poured towards the gates but there seemed to be no signage or control measures to get the tribes moving in the right direction. People were carried along in the flow past the gate they needed for entry and into a confused press as they were refused entry at another gate. They started to swim back against the tide pressing forward. The handful of supporters of Australia or their opponents Fiji were conspicuous in their team strips in a sea of French mufti. They called out to each other in English passing along information about where the gates were located and how the entry security system worked. It was all a little too chaotic for us. Everyone was good-humoured and took the confusion in their stride, but this might not have been the case if a local team, or more frighteningly, two local teams, had been playing. We soon realised that crowd control was not a French long-suit and made a resolution to get to the game in Bordeaux much earlier.

Inside the stadium it was a lacklustre affair and the Wallabies won comfortably over a flat Fijian outfit. We braved the tram crowd back to town and scurried back to Sète as fast as we could.

We had a layover day to do the regular tourist stuff in Sète and find an internet connection, and the Med coast was done and dusted. We got back onto the bike and took to the mountain roads heading for the Atlantic coast and the last pool game in Bordeaux. Rolling towards the hinterland on the crisp cool morning of 25 September we felt refreshed after our short break in Sète. We had under-dressed for the morning believing that the sun would burn off the cloud cover and warm the day as it had each morning over the previous week, but as we climbed into the mountains the temperature plummeted. By the late morning coffee-stop at Mazamet we were ready for more clothing and a neck warmer to keep out the chill. The Indian summer was over (or, at least, gone back to India for the weekend). We knew from bitter experience just how miserable life could get on a motorbike in the winter and we could smell the cold waiting for us just up ahead.

Restricting ourselves to a 320-kilometre ride on the back roads, the journey to Argen through the mountains was a delight. There were endless sweeping corners, with an excellent hard dry surface. Even the car drivers seemed determined to make it enjoyable for the tourists, moving over to allow us to slide past. The bike was handling beautifully and I had the feeling that we were moving smoothly and gracefully through the turns. This fantasy only lasted until I looked across to see our shadow against a cutting wall and realised that in profile the Beemer looked like a praying mantis: all elbows, knees and bulbous bits. Whatever we were, we were not graceful.

We selected a west coast tourist town as our base for the Bordeaux game and sauntered into Arcachon on 26 September. Located an hour west of Bordeaux on the Atlantic coast, it had plenty of accommodation in late September and we had no problem finding an apartment for a week at a fair price. Like many seaside tourist towns, Arcachon had a genteel seediness about it. The ramshackle casino and faded grand houses that fronted the lake on which it was built had their heyday when people went on holidays by train and life, even on holidays, was an altogether more formal business. Late in the season, the boardwalks, jetties and sidewalk cafés were almost empty and we didn't have to wait for a table anywhere. With the brooding Atlantic a few kilometres west over the sand hills, the weather was threatening and the leaden sky and early winter rains convinced us we had arrived none too soon. Many places were starting to close for the long winter hibernation.

With a few days to spare, we toured the vineyards north of Bordeaux. This is the home of the famous Margaux and Médoc wines. It is a very pretty area, in that 'ordered vineyard' way that is now very familiar all over the world, and touristy in a way that is also sadly familiar. There are over 5000 châteaux and 57 'appellations' in this area. Wines with the good housekeeping seal of approval have 'AOC' on the label indicating the tick of the *Appellation d'Origine Contrôlée*. We decided that this is all you need to know to have a good time around Bordeaux, provided you don't get run over by a tourist bus.

The Bordeaux wines include some excellent full-bodied reds that appeal to our taste. Despite the temptation of cellar door sales, however, we generally settled for €5 cheapies at the equivalent of a liquor barn and found them quite drinkable with our cheap meals. The budget thanked us for the effort. We had only been on the road for a month and we were struggling with prices and hopelessly overspending.

We caught the train up to Bordeaux and sat in heavy rain to watch the Wallabies run all over an outclassed Canadian outfit then caught the first train straight back. Our rainy day in Bordeaux showed us nothing useful about the place except that we could find a warm café and an indulgent pastry on a cold wet day. But this was hardly a revelation in France.

On the Sunday after the game, Nick packed up his little rental car and headed north to Paris to return it before lunch on Monday. He was heading back to the UK. We would see him again in late October in Oxford but we were both sad to see him go. It was the offspring growing to adulthood and establishing their own lives that had allowed us to take some different roads but we still missed having them around; missed their good company and good counsel. Both of them had always been more grown up than us in some ways.

After Nick made a break for the hills, Jo and I settled in for a few more days. The weather improved and then reverted to rain. We knew that it was now early October, well into autumn, and that the weather would just get more cantankerous from here forward. We fitted the liners into our riding jackets and spent some time working out how we could pack more warm clothing on the bike. From here we were planning to go north again into colder weather in the Loire and Champagne regions, Belgium, Paris and then back to England for Sarah and Mike's wedding. This seemed like the wrong time of year to be going in this direction but we reckoned we would work out how to deal with the cold weather as we travelled. It was a good theory!

Our holiday by the Atlantic ran out as quickly as the last good weather. One last walk around the village to check on the locals and we were riding north to the Loire Valley. Located about 200 kilometres south of Paris, this is the location of the picture-book châteaux that look so romantic on postcards. The run up was about 480 kilometres, the weather overcast and it rained most of the day but we made better time than expected and hauled into Blois by mid-afternoon.

Blois (magnificently pronounced Blwah) is roughly in the centre of the château district of the Loire Valley. It is a small town of about 20,000 souls. The city has its own château, not wanting to be outdone, and a well-preserved historical centre. There were also some wonderful public gardens setting off the buildings. In the French style, the gardens tortured nature to unnatural perfection. They were clipped and manicured, with trees trained to the point of plant abuse; beautiful, but to our antipodean eyes, surreally unnatural.

We chose to visit only two of the dozen or so open châteaux. The first was Château de Cheverny. The building was magnificent and, as it had been occupied as a family home until 1985, had very complete furnishings. The workmanship in both the building and the furniture was excellent and reflected the quality of the craft system within France. Cheverny also maintained a pack of about 100 hunting dogs that were of particular interest to Jo. These huge, long-legged hounds, a cross between the British Terrier and the French Poitevin, looked at Jo longingly through the kennel bars with eyes that could only be saying 'hello entree!' The second château, at Chenonceau, was equally well built and presented. The gardens, in particular, were very impressive, although 16th and 17th Century French gardeners certainly flogged nature into line. Thousands of folk must have got a payday out of the competition between the nobles to have the most impressive display.

For the few days in the Loire, we cruised around the back roads having a great time on the bike with the weight of our luggage back at our digs. We quickly worked out that the best time to be on the roads in rural France was in the early afternoon when every self-respecting rural Frenchman was at home eating something cooked in duck fat or in his local restaurant scoffing the *plat du jour*. Things started to get going again after about 3pm, by which time we could be finished with our touristic endeavours and looking to our own vittles. We had adapted quickly to French food and found how to eat healthy meals that were not too expensive. We had always taken great care with our diet at home and we did not want to fall into bad eating habits on the road. From the start we carried a small cooler box with food for daily consumption and emergency use. It produced an endless supply of fruit, yoghurt, bread and cheese which took care of breakfast and lunch. Interestingly, Jo had been concerned about her cholesterol level for a while and initially steered away from the wonderful cheeses. After watching me demolish a whole roll of goat's cheese for lunch, she rationalized that, unlike cheese, French *fromage* was low in cholesterol and OK to eat. After that I had to share.

We did have, of course, a few misadventures. One evening we wandered into a small café feeling very pleased with the world and looking forward to a hearty meal to round off a good day. We ordered on the basis of the waiter's recommendation, without consulting the menu, and it was about here that our day's ration of luck ran out. The food was stodgy and tasteless and gave the distinct impression of having been sitting around waiting for our arrival since morning, our wine glasses were poorly serviced and the waiter was just plain rude. We ate our meal but the fun had evaporated from our day. When the bill arrived, however, it was at least twice the fair price of our meal. We remonstrated with a blank faced waiter who just shrugged his shoulders and insisted that the price was the price. We paid and left, grumpy that we had been stung and, as the initial shock of the confrontation wore off, angry with ourselves that we hadn't stood our ground more firmly in the face of such a bare-faced scam. We determined that we wouldn't be done over so easily again.

It was now well into the autumn and we were away from the

moderating maritime climate of the coastal towns. It was starting to get cold at night and cool enough during the shortening days to keep us well rugged up on the bike. Despite this, at the end of our Loire Valley stopover we were travelling well and had most of the technical stuff on the bike sorted. We still needed a little more stowage to take care of some bulky cold weather gear for the weeks ahead. Otherwise the first 5000 kilometres had been trouble free. When it came time to leave the Loire, we roared straight up the motorway from Blois. We had been slower getting away than planned and needed to be at the next stop in Troyes by 12.30pm to find some accommodation before everything closed down for the long lunch. Needing to make about even-time (averaging 100 km/h) for the trip, we paid our money on the motorway and opened up the throttle. It wasn't long before Jo was explaining exponential equations as we watched the fuel gauge expire before our eyes. 15 percent more speed was costing us a 40 percent penalty in fuel. At 140 km/h you could almost see the fuel gauge move as you glanced at it. Clearly we had the aerodynamics of a barn door. At home, a day of mixed riding would get an easy 500 kilometres from the 30 litre tank. With this load on board we got about 400 to a tank on the motorway if we kept the cruise at 120. Over 140, the little 'feed me now' light came on at about 280 kilometres. The problem with this was that 95-octane petrol cost about US$2.50 per litre, or better than US$50 every time we filled the tank! The only saving grace was that at high speed you would run out of country after a couple of days. We had a tight budget for this trip, however, and we didn't want to miss out on a decent bistro meal for the sake of a quicker trip up the motorway. So we established some simple rules: stay off the motorway, take a little longer on the back lanes, and if you have to get onto the motorway (or the better A roads) stay under 120 km/h no matter how good the road and how light the traffic.

Interestingly, we didn't see many fast sports bikes on the motorways but there were a few big, fast super-tourers. The Honda ST1300s, BMW GTs and Yamaha XJR 1300s generally had a couple on board in matching leathers and helmets with full and very neat luggage fit. They slid by at about 150 tucked in behind the big fairings. We watched them go with a wave and told ourselves that the decision to bring the BMW GSA would pay off later when the roads got bad and the distances got longer.

Leaving the Loire marked a change in the way we felt about our journey. Up until then we had felt a little like frauds, pretending to be off on a journey, while really just mucking about on a bike. Our conversations with others were cautious. We had never been straightforward about our ambitions and kept our plans vague and ill-defined. But somewhere in the Loire we started to feel settled on the road. Our organisation had improved to the point where most of the stress had gone from our day-to-day lives. The bike and the luggage fit had worked out well and we had at least recognised the shortcomings of the set-up and learnt how to cope. Our confidence was growing and at last we felt our journey had really started. We continued to be reluctant to talk about where we hoped our journey would take us but we knew that, at last, it had begun.

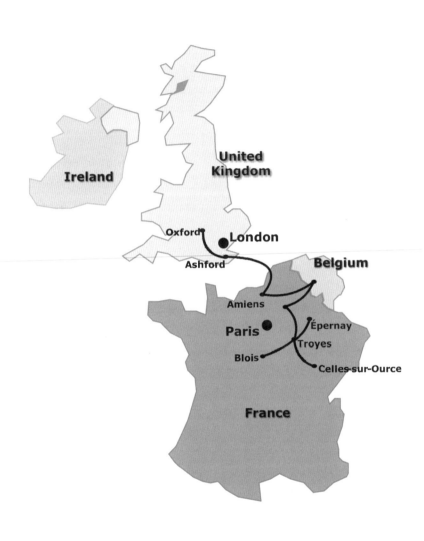

Ireland

United
Kingdom

Oxford
London
Ashford

Belgium

Amiens

Paris

Épernay
Troyes

Blois

Celles-sur-Ource

France

3

Elephant Gets a Name

We got into Troyes early enough to have a light lunch and get out on our feet to explore. Troyes is a modern French city grown up around a well-preserved medieval city centre. It is the capital of the Aube *département* of the Champagne region and has been an important place since medieval times. Since 1505, it had been the capital of the French hosiery industry and was home to Lacoste knitwear. Perhaps because of this, it was claimed to be Europe's biggest factory outlet centre (noting our distinct lack of luggage space we didn't check the validity of the claim). Rebuilt in the Middle Ages after a great fire, the town centre forms an attractive tourist precinct with buildings preserved or restored to maintain the medieval look and feel of the place. Improvements in the sewage and waste disposal systems have, thankfully, brought the smell of the narrow alleys up to date.

Troyes also produced 25 percent of France's sauerkraut! I found this apparently random piece of information in a tourist brochure just before we sat down to one of those long French lunches. Inspired, I ordered the local delicacy as part of the usual four-course set menu. The plate that arrived was huge. It was covered with a thick padding of sauerkraut with two fat sausages loitering on top. This, I determined, must have been a test of French machismo so I ordered a second carafe of the house rosé and set to work. After a manful effort I had washed down the sausages and a small portion of my mountain of sauerkraut and sat staring at the remainder while Jo joked that there would be no pastry with my coffee that day. I pushed the plate away with the vow not to bother with pickled cabbage again. Of course, later in this journey we would push far to the north and east of this continent to places where root vegetables and preserved cabbage are staples and to go without cabbage is to go hungry.

After a little investigation of the town, we decided it was well located for exploring the wineries of the Champagne region to the north east and south east. We considered that such important work needed time, so we found a small farmhouse that we could rent for a week at a village located on the vast rolling plains of Champagne about 16 kilometres east of Troyes called Buoy-Luxembourg. Neither our landlady nor her husband (nor probably anyone else in the village) could speak any English, but we managed to find the place, do the deal, and move in without much difficulty.

The soil of Champagne is clay-chalk and was not much use for agriculture until the introduction of artificial fertilizers. These days, the locals grow huge tracts of sugar beets, subsidized by the EU. No-one there would even consider why they are growing sugar in such an inefficient way when it could come out of South America at one tenth of the price. French support for the heritage of its rural roots is deep-seated and goes largely unquestioned. The idea of agribusinesses would be anathema to most of these farming communities where the farms remain family smallholdings based on the well ordered life of the French village.

Buoy-Luxembourg looked much like hundreds of other villages in this area. The locals had a good quality of life, thanks to the EU

Common Agricultural Policy and it seemed to us outsiders like a reasonable place to live… if you like small towns. The houses were large and well insulated with large yards, most with vegetable gardens and chicken or pheasant runs. The farm machinery was modern and well maintained. The local junior school looked smart and well appointed. Even the dogs looked well fed. Using the village as a base, we were able to explore far and wide over the Champagne region. We went to wineries in both the northern Marne and southern Aube *départements,* and spent some time in Troyes exploring some of its less well-know attractions.

The major Champagne appellations are located an hour's ride north east of Troyes. Every year thousands of tourists flock to the village of Épernay, 25 kilometres south of Reims in northern France, to visit the great champagne houses gathered along the avenue de Champagne. Even on the cool autumn day we visited, well out of the tourist season, there were enough visitors for the cellar tours to depart every 20 minutes at the Moët et Chandon headquarters. Our group had about 15 English speakers, with UK, US and Australian accents. As we looked around, there wasn't much about the wine on display. Most of the promotional material was directed at an apparently enviable lifestyle that included lots of Moët; with posters of beautiful young things with perfect smiles telling us that champagne is sophisticated. This should have been a clear indication about what was to follow but we waited with considerable anticipation for our insight into champagne production regardless.

Soon we were being guided by a young man, named Julian, with a soft French accent dressed in the corporate uniform of black suit, black shirt and black tie. He ushered us into a small theatre to sit through an in-house video that set the tone with slick production but no useful information. We then followed him through parts of the 28 kilometres of cellar tunnels set aside for tourists. Julian explained how champagne *was* made emphasizing hand turning of bottles and long family traditions. Skipped over in the presentation was the simple fact that champagne is now made like any other modern wine: fermented in huge stainless steel vats in an industrial shed then turned and purged by machines. It has been made this way since the 1960s and it would be impossible to make a million bottles a year any other way. Under questioning Julian admitted that the family no longer controlled the company, which had been part of a conglomerate since the 1980s, though we were assured that the family values still drove the company. We visited the tasting room for our one glass of the product before being abandoned in the boutique with the expectation that we would buy a bottle or two to take away with us. We rushed out into the cool autumn afternoon and left without looking back, sure that we had just been given an 1-hour long advertisement for the champagne lifestyle and paid US$20 for the privilege. We were very disappointed. We had, after all, come for the wine. All we had discovered was that Épernay is the centre of a French marketing marvel that has sold wine with bubbles as a lifestyle accessory for 90 years.

A visit to the great champagne houses, however, is not the whole story of the district or this great wine style. While 75 percent of the vineyards legally allowed to provide grapes for true champagne lie in the Marne *département* around Reims and Épernay, the other 25 percent is situated more than 120 kilometres south in the *département* of Aube. The wine growing area in Aube is more limited and centres on about 20 villages from Les Riceys in the south to Bar-sur-Aube 30 kilometres to the north-east. The

Aube wineries have a long history of champagne production but when the areas for inclusion in Champagne's *Appellation d'Origine Contrôlée* (AOC) were established in 1909 the Aube *département* vineyards were not included. Eighteen years of conflict, including crippling strikes and confrontation followed. The chaos was such that the Army was brought in to regain government control. By the time the dispute was settled and Aube was included in the areas of the Champagne AOC, the major producers of the north had established market dominance in a new, image-driven, wine market. As a consequence, the southern wineries had missed their place in the champagne marketing juggernaut, but that didn't diminish the quality of their product or the experience of a visit.

The day after visiting Épernay, we rode south and selected a winery at Celles-sur-Ource, on the basis that it advertised that English was spoken. We pulled the bike up onto its stand on the footpath near the door of Champagne Marcel Vézien unannounced. It was a bitterly cold foggy day and customers were thin on the ground. The locals complained that it was unseasonable weather but we suspected that they were just being polite to visitors!

This was a genuine family business run by Jean-Pierre and Marie-José Vézien. There was no charge for tours or tasting and we settled into the warmth of the tasting bar with Marie-José for a chat about the history of the vineyard and the wines. There were no special areas in the buildings dedicated to tourists and the image of the product or the company. The business went on around us. Jean-Pierre wandered through in work clothes for a chat.

It was just a short walk to the wine-making sheds to see the process underway and get an understanding of how this wine is made in the 21st Century. Here in Celles-sur-Ource, whatever was done with the wine once it was in the bottle was far less important than making a quality wine to begin with. This was first and foremost a wine-making business.

We selected three champagnes for tasting, a chardonnay, a pinot noir and a rosé, and tasted them in that order with the stronger rosé last. All had strong varietal character, interest and complexity. We purchased two bottles of the rosé to take with us for friends in Belgium and a bottle of the chardonnay for that evening. Our host packed them in boxes for transport on the bike and threw in a reusable stopper, a pen, a key ring and a smile.

That night we enjoyed our champagne with a simple home cooked meal in the warmth of our rented farmhouse and talked about what we had discovered. Somewhere between the marketing triumph of the Épernay houses and the small family vineyards of the Aube was a more complex and reassuring story than we had anticipated. To visit one was to find champagne as a lifestyle accessory prized for its brand name and exclusivity. To visit the other was to get involved with the wine for its own sake. We sipped our wine, content with the thought that there was a limit to how sophisticated a lifestyle two desperados on a motorbike could have.

Being static for a week was also a great chance to be domestic for a while. We were able to do some overdue maintenance on some of our equipment and shopping and cooking for ourselves in a proper kitchen was a treat. We also kept away from the usual tourist France (the wineries excepted) and thoroughly enjoyed meeting ordinary French people while watching the world go by from our little village. We were also beginning to discover that one of the delights of being an independent traveller is finding the unexpected. Sometimes it is a small bar, warm on a cold day, where the locals embrace the traveller and tell you their special secrets.

Sometimes it is a small museum or local history overlooked by the rest of the world. Our wanders through the back streets of Troyes turned up just such a gem.

Hidden down a narrow street, at 7 rue de la Trinité, the Maison de l'Outil et de la Pensée Ouvrière (the Museum of Hand Tools) is announced with a small sign easily overlooked by the passer-by. The building itself dates from 1556 and was the family home of a rich merchant, Jean Mauroy. Jean and his wife, Louise de Pleures, died without children and willed their estate to provide a college for young orphans. The administrators of the estate established a workshop to produce knitted stockings that allowed the orphans to follow an apprenticeship as textile workers. It eventually became the most important manufactory in Troyes. In 1969, the City gave the building over to the establishment of a tool museum and library. The Museum welcomed its first visitors in 1974. In the intervening years the Museum building has been restored and the collection developed. It now displays hand tools used by all of the important trades from the 18th and 19th Centuries; the time before mechanization. The number of trades represented is amazing: carpenters, stonecutters, tilers, brick makers, farriers, masons, coopers, blacksmiths, furriers, millstone dressers, glove makers, clog makers and many more find space in the galleries. Like many of these small museums in France this one is beautifully presented. The display cases are well laid out, well lit and uncluttered enough to display the exhibits clearly. Our €6.50 admission gave us use of a folder with the numbered exhibits named in English which was very useful for some of the more esoteric items. For me, the visit to the tool museum was a telling counterpoint to our visits to the grand châteaux of the Loire Valley. The tools are practical but simple and seem, to our modern eyes, to be too primitive to have produced the beautifully crafted buildings and furniture of the châteaux. But used by craftsmen of great skill these tools were enough to build both the beauty and excesses of the châteaux and thousands of less spectacular but equally elegant items of everyday life.

It was mid-October by the time we left Buoy-Luxembourg riding the deserted back roads north-west on a clear Sunday. The weather was turning cold and the thought of spending a winter out on the frozen plains of Champagne was unappealing. The hunting season had only opened a week before and every kilometre or so a shooter walked through the cropped fields with a shotgun over his shoulder and a dog bounding along behind. Sunday is a Frenchman's day to hunt and a good day for small birds and furry animals to lay low.

Our destination was Laon, an ancient citadel town and seat of power. We saw it 30 kilometres out rising abruptly 100 metres above the plain on a hard limestone outcrop with the spires of its 12th Century cathedral stark against a powder blue sky. The site provided a natural defensive position that dominated the surrounding plain; the perfect spot to rule a kingdom. The Carolingian Kings knew a good thing and made it their capital for 150 years until 987AD. From the plain below, the citadel with its spired cathedral and heavily fortified walls must have been an impressive sight to the peasants toiling in the fields.

Our arrival at the old city corresponded with the running of *le Circuit d'Remparts*. This annual fun run is a community event based around the old city and has categories for young 'uns over 500 metres, codgers over 3300 metres and the young guns over 10 kilometres. Part of the old city was blocked off for the event but we were able to park and walk in without difficulty. While negotiating the barricades, we realised that this was the third town that we had arrived in to coincide with a fun run. The cool, stable weather of autumn was obviously the time for these events, but it was impressive that they are commonplace across the land.

The old city was interesting, but a little tired looking. It seemed that many of the businesses had moved to the newer area 'downtown', as the locals called it, and a new economy had yet to develop 'uptown'. Still, it was a lovely place and we found ourselves looking in the real estate office windows at the price of the better houses with great views along the edge of the town and calculating the price in Australian dollars. This is always a sign that we are impressed. The best part of our visit to Laon, however, started in a car park. We had arrived, locked up the bike and were busy orientating the map when we were approached by a couple and asked if we needed help. Jean and Françoise were locals, proud of their town and keen for visitors to enjoy it. We struck up a conversation that ended with us being invited to their home for drinks that evening. We accepted without hesitation and found a delightful chocolate shop where Jo bought some local specialties with champagne liqueur centres so that we didn't arrive empty handed. Jean and Françoise were wonderful hosts and talking, drinking and eating went on far later than we anticipated. Françoise turned out to be a history and English language teacher who spoke the lingo with a beautiful soft accent. We found out all manner of wonderful local information and enjoyed their company very much.

The next day, and against common sense, we continued to travel north from Laon into cooler and wetter weather. We were travelling north to see some old friends now living in Belgium and it would have taken more than a little chill to keep us away.

We had decided, for no particular reason, to spend a night in Brussels on the way to our next stop. A number of our friends and acquaintances had been posted there for work over the years and we felt we should have a look at the place for ourselves. So, we charged across the Belgium border and ploughed into the city an hour later. The first thing we noticed was that there were few, if any, bikes and the drivers were hopeless compared with the ever-courteous French. We had ridden and driven in some of the worst traffic in the world over the years and, by our measure, Brussels didn't rate as a congested city. The drivers, however, were keen to make up for the lack of volume and chaos by a lack of manners. Although I was starting to feel a little more comfortable and a little less clumsy, riding the fully laden BMW in any city remained a challenge. Jo had started to recognise the signs that I was fully focussed on riding. I would stop talking on the intercom, for one thing, or start to talk to myself coaching each new riding action. Sometimes it must have seemed a little bizarre:

'Down a gear…down a gear…stay wide stupid…stay wide, stay wide! That's it, turn hard now…power on… power on, damn! Up we come! More power you bastard!'

This day we were both busy on the intercom, Jo sorting the navigation and me trying to avoid terminally stupid Belgian drivers, when I was forced to swerve violently to avoid a vehicle that had simply driven into our path with no right of way. 'Idiot!,' I cried, swerving around the curb side and poking the raised middle finger of my left hand at the driver. 'Riding this mongrel is like riding an elephant!'

'Ah, I don't know,' said Jo. 'The elephants I've seen did pretty much what the mahouts wanted.'

'Yeah,' I responded. 'But that was only because the elephants didn't have anything else on that day.'

It was a corny joke but good enough to break the tension and keep us entertained deciding what alternative arrangements elephants might have on any particular day. Going to the hairdresser didn't seem to work for an elephant, but waxing seemed about right.

'Not right now, mate. I'm off to get the waxing done,' says the elephant as she pitches the mahout into the river.

By the time we finished the elephant jokes we had decided that Brussels wasn't our town and there was no particular reason to be there. It was about then that a warning light for brake failure flashed up on the dash.

'This bloody elephant's got stuffed brakes,' I cried, and pulled into a service station. A quick check of the brake system didn't show up any obvious problems and the warning light extinguished when we started off again. Still, it was something else to worry about.

We headed out of town to look at another part of Belgium. We settled on Waterloo. The main attraction at Waterloo is, of course, the site of the famous battle that saw the last defeat of the Emperor Napoleon. Unfortunately we found the tourist sites to be in a poor state of repair. The main feature was a statue of a lion, facing towards Paris, erected by the victorious Wellington on the top of an artificial hill. This act of hubris by the victors set the tone of European relations for the next 80 years. We declined to pay the €6 entrance fee to the monument and wandered around the high hedge grown to block the view from cheapskates like us. On the back side we saw a rabbit head under the hedge and investigated to find a tunnel. We climbed through, had a look, took a photo, and climbed back the way we had come. In the field next to the Lion on the Hill there was second man-made mound. This one was a huge pile of EU subsidized sugar beet waiting to be collected. We reckoned that this was a much more poignant monument; a mundane counterpoint to hubristic excess.

That night we wandered the near-deserted streets of Waterloo looking for some cheap eats. There wasn't much on offer so we settled on a Lebanese Café in the main street. The place had some old black and white photos of Beirut on the wall. When we took an interest in them we struck up a conversation with the couple who owned the place. They had left The Lebanon at the start of the civil war and, since I had been in Beirut in the last days of that war, we had enough common ground to get a good chat going. This unexpected bonhomie must have lowered our guard. We accepted the cook's recommendation and opted for stuffed eggplant, which was the plat du jour. I say lowered our guard because we had made it a habit not to eat the plat du jour so late in the day when it had been sitting around since morning. There was always something that needed to be cooked fresh on every menu. Besides, the state of the cook's filthy fingernails should have been a giveaway! Whatever the cause of our oversight, the consequence was clear shortly after we arrived at our friends' Bob and Bronny's place in the village of Jurbise the next day. Jo spent two of our three days there laid low with a mild case of food poisoning; timing perfect. For my part I got away with some stomach cramps and minor discomfort, a fact I put down to flushing the system out with several litres of Belgian beer. I was careful not to be too smug, however, as I knew my time would come.

It rained for two days while we were in Belgium so we were happy to find a dry road for the run back to France where we had one remaining European stop before returning to the UK for our daughter's wedding. The city of Amiens lay 150 kilometres south in the *départment* of the Somme and is the site of some important WWI battlefields. From a neat and warm hotel in the middle of town we discovered another wonderful little French city. One of Amiens' claims to fame is it has the biggest cathedral in France. Being France it was, of course, called Notre Dame as are most other French cathedrals including the one in Paris. This gothic monster, however, would swallow up two of the Paris version.

Two nights in Amiens allowed us to visit Villers-Bretonneux and the nearby Australian Memorial. Villers-Bretonneux was completely destroyed in what they called the Great War, although my grandfather, who fought at the nearby Mont St-Quentin, once pointed out to me that there was nothing *great* about it. The Franco-Australian Museum in the Victoria School was modest and well presented. It has some excellent photos and a few quality exhibits. It was well worth our €4 entry and we stayed until the attendant told us she was closing to take the mandatory long French lunch. Feeling like lunch ourselves, we headed out to the nearby Australian Memorial and parked the bike in front of one of the impressive porticos that mark the entry. Armed with our lunch box we headed up into the cemetery section of the area and found a bench to spread out our bread, cheese, ham and wine. Out of the wind and in the sun, the memorial was a beautiful place and was clearly intended to inspire contemplation. We munched away and contemplated.

While we were there three men with a taxi waiting moved quickly around the memorial and departed. An older gentleman walked through as quickly as he was able, puffed up to the top of the memorial tower to take a photo before rushing away to his waiting taxi. A young man moved through quickly but stopped to share some wine and bread with us before rushing off with a glance at his watch. As we packed our modest lunch and continued with our visit two women arrived and stomped through at the double march. They spent less than 5 minutes in the park and when I spoke to one of them she said she had to rush because they must be someplace else sometime soon. She left with the parting remark that 'they were all so young'. Jo and I were left a little unsettled by all this. Surely this place is not the type of tourist attraction that you could collect like a stamp. Why would you come if you couldn't spend even a few minutes thinking about what it all means? The final insult for me was the comment about the age of the soldiers. This was a cliché mindlessly repeated. If this person had really looked at the grave stones she would have seen that, far from being a field of callow youths, this was a graveyard of mature men. Had she thought about this for a few minutes she might have realised that whatever might have been the naïve enthusiasm of the 1915 landing on Gallipoli, it must have been replaced by something else by 1918 when the great battles that ended the war on the Western Front were fought. One thing was for sure, the small Army that triumphed at Amiens was no lamb being led to slaughter. It was well trained, hardened, experienced and professional. It was also brilliantly led by the Melbourne engineer John Monash. Its battles were won through detailed planning and rehearsal with nothing left to chance. These troops, fighting on the far side of their world, were the first to master the detailed coordination of all the disparate forces in a modern battle. It is a great story, much more uplifting than a claim to sad victim-hood, and it deserves better understanding than it got this day. We rode back to Amiens grumbling about 'bloody Australians', and we weren't talking about those long gone hard-men of 1918.

By this stage the Rugby World Cup had finally run it course

but, with our team knocked out in the quarter-finals, we had not gone to the expense of seeking out tickets to the elimination matches. We had also decided to avoid Paris in Rugby World Cup Finals week and save that city for another (warmer) time. With our daughter holed-up in London for the foreseeable future, there would hopefully be a few more opportunities.

With more than six weeks of travel behind us we were starting to understand the beauty of being truly independent travellers. Our five weeks in France were over but there was still much we didn't understand about this country. Clearly, we would have to come back.

We left Amiens in the wet pre-dawn fog on the morning of 22 October heading towards Calais, the Channel Tunnel and our return to the United Kingdom. The road was slippery, jammed with traffic and detoured around accidents in several places. Nonetheless, we were getting the hang of European conditions. We left our grim, determined faces packed with the luggage and chatted quietly even as we could feel the back wheel spin and the bike slide around on the wet clay detours.

We felt like old hands crossing through the Channel Tunnel and we rolled out onto the left-hand side of the English motorway by mid morning, found some cheap (relatively) accommodation in the town of Ashford in Kent, and started straight into a list of administrative tasks that needed attention. For the next three days we sourced bike spares, used the internet and dealt with a dozen other major and minor jobs needed to keep us on the road.

We used a small travel computer to launch a steady stream of email messages aimed at keeping in touch with our friends and family. Some weeks, finding the energy to write was a chore. Finding an internet connection was also a problem, especially in the UK. Most of the cheaper places we stayed at either didn't have any internet connection or had a commercial arrangement with a supplier that required us to purchase time at a ridiculous rate. We started to carry our tiny computer everywhere with us and keep it switched on looking 'stray electrons'. When we found a WiFi connection unsecured, we sat down any place we could and made the best of it to check our mail and make calls using Voice Over Internet Protocol (VOIP).

We had trouble finding such a connection in Ashford until a local informed us that there were some free computers in the Government shopfront. We found the place quickly and found the two computers with free internet but both were being used and there were people waiting for access.

'Do you have WiFi?' asked Jo.

'What's that, love?' came the response from the lady behind the desk.

'You know, wireless internet so we could use our own computer,' Jo continued. The desk lady looked a little confused, but by this time I had the top up on my computer and had found an unsecured signal that was strong and clear.

'Here it is. Do you mind if we sit down and use this?'

She still looked a little confused but indicated the waiting area. We plonked ourselves down in two of the dozen seats arranged in a horseshoe around a small coffee table covered with waiting-room magazines. For the next two and a half hours, until our computer's battery finally gave out, we did our banking, paid our bills, answered our mail, phoned our parents and booked some tickets to the Moto GP in Valencia, Spain, scheduled for 11 November.

Throughout this, a parade of locals slouched through the

The bike ready to ship. It was waiting for us in one piece when we arrived in London.

Luggage for a year, with sidebags for wet weather gear and water etc.

Wembley, London. The bike fully packed for the first time after several hours trying to get everything to fit.

The wet weather gear was always close at hand in the UK.

Jo and Sarah looking glamorous for Sarah's wedding near Oxford...

...And a very different Jo two days later, during a rest-stop in the Pyrenees.

Morocco offered spectacular, tough country: Anti Atlas Mountains...

...and spectacular, tough riding: Dadès Gorge.

On the Tizi n'Tichka Pass, heading for Marrakech. A few days without snow meant an easy, pleasant ride.

Sheep on their way to market for the festival of sacrifice.

Shopping in the Rabat *kasbah*.

In Morocco, Elephant was a giant.

How big? How heavy? How fast?

Using sign language to solve a problem.   The English bookshop in Rabat.

Elephant secure, off the street and out of sight.

Elephant handled the Moroccan Sahara like a... camel.

The village of Oualidia, where our trip nearly ended due to Jo's back injury.

Moroccan mopeds have a hard life.

This cosy two-seater at Bulla Regia...

...could not compete with this 12-seat model for 'public convenience'.

waiting area looking for help with benefits or advice for everything from unemployment to teenage pregnancy. From the young to the senior citizens, they sized us up and took a great interest in what these two strangers in their black riding suits were up to. With sideways glances from behind magazines and ears cocked to hear what we were saying, they watched and listened to us intently. At first we were embarrassed by the attention and spoke to each other in a whisper, but with so much to do and the battery-clock running down relentlessly, we eventually forgot about the audience and just got on with it. We didn't know what these folk thought about the performance and didn't care too much, but the experience triggered some interesting feelings. For the first time we saw the unasked question standing in the corner like a forlorn elephant: 'Whatever planet you're from, why do you get to do what you do, while I get to sit here waiting for the government?'. We would see variations of this sad eyed question many times and, of course, there is no sensible answer to it. We did then what we would continue to do. We smiled and went about our business, remaining steadfastly thankful for our own good fortune.

Our three days in Ashford were busy apart from our internet tasks. By now we had learned that when you are on the road, stuff wears out and breaks. Keeping on top of the maintenance was a constant battle that sometimes required a little ingenuity. I had two problems with my helmet that needed a fix. The first was a broken intercom harness, which meant that neither of the women in my life (Jo and Kylie) could be heard inside the helmet. Under some circumstances this may have been a good thing but, since Kylie and Jo did the navigating, we found life without an intercom difficult. The second was a problem with air blasting into the bottom of the helmet at high speed. This seemed to be caused by the luggage-fit which had changed the flow of air around the front of the bike. This was not a huge problem when the temperature was warm, but in the cold weather my eyes were starting to become irritated. I managed to get a replacement helmet loom from the BMW dealer in Royal Tunbridge Wells and fitting it up took an hour. First problem solved. For problem two I purchased an old nylon bag at a junk shop for 50p and cut out two flaps of 100-denier Cordura for the underside of the chin section of the helmet. Lengths of hook and loop tape (part of our spares kit) were sewn onto the overlap and the sections were super-glued into the helmet. This worked well and kept the cold draughts out most of the time.

After three days in Ashford, we had our administration sorted and were on our way up to Oxford for our daughter Sarah's wedding. It rained all the way but we were getting used to the weather and breezed through the trip without too much discomfort. Sarah had booked us into a very luxurious B&B near the centre of Oxford and after some of the places we had been staying, Jo was pleased to see the king-sized bed! There was enough room in the suite to hold a dance party if we could have found a band.

As expected, Oxford was full of students and bicycles and canals full of punts unused in the autumn chill. On Friday 26 October our son Nick and John Green (father of the groom) turned up and moved into rooms in the same B&B. We had last seen Nick in Arcachon on France's Atlantic coast and John in Carmarthen in Wales. The four of us trundled off to a local pub for dinner and a quick catch up on all that had happened in the intervening weeks.

Sarah and Mike had met when they both worked for the same law firm in Sydney. They moved to the UK after Mike's mother had a stroke and survived but remained seriously ill. As an only child, Mike returned to support his dad and both Jo and I took this as a measure of the man. Sarah moved to the UK with him and they started to carve out a life and plan a future in a tiny apartment in inner London. The bride and groom had organised their own wedding, determined to do what they wanted on their day. Jo and I had done the same thing 32 years before, although on a much more modest budget, and we strongly approved of their stand. It gave us confidence that they understood that the ceremony was just a milestone on a longer adventure and not an end in itself.

Saturday 27 October 2007 was the day of the wedding. After wearing nothing but riding suits and travel clothes for weeks, dressing up was a strange experience but we scrubbed up pretty well. It was a small gathering with only a few close friends and intimate family and, as requested by the invitation, the ladies looked 'glamorous' and the men 'dashing'.

In a few hours it was all over. We retreated to our B&B, sipped a glass of wine and let it sink in. Our daughter, long since her own woman, brought up to be independent, but still our dear first-born, was married.

'That's it,' I said. 'There's nothing else we can show them.'

'We can show them how to grow old,' Jo replied, always the wise counsel on these matters.

We had booked a return passage on the Channel Tunnel train for the evening of 28 October, the day following the wedding. The newly wed couple was departing on their honeymoon on the same day and our son was returning to London. We packed our gear and got ready for the next stage of our journey. It was cold and wet and the winter was close by. There was no longer any reason to stay.

We rode south through the rain, fast.

Ireland

United Kingdom

Oxford • London

Calais

Belgium

Paris

Orléans

France

Montauban

Zaragoza

Portugal

Spain

Barcelona

Jerez de la Fontera

Granada

Calpe

Algeciras

4

Spain, Home and Back

Some days are just merciless. Still emotional after Sarah and Mike's wedding, and a little sad at saying goodbye to Sarah, Mike and Nick, our run to the Channel Tunnel was always going to be an ordinary day. When it started raining heavily during breakfast we put on our resigned, determined faces and broke out the wet weather kit.

Although our riding suits are '100 percent waterproof', bitter experience had taught us that the '100 percent' part of this standard is negotiable. As a consequence we carried a fully waterproof outer layer for the seriously wet days. Apart from the pants and coat, this included a pair of over-boots to keep the little pinkies dry. We didn't like wearing our wet weather gear because it was too hot. But this day there was no alternative. We pulled on our gear and got out in the rain before we expired. The rain swirled and buffeted around the trucks on the motorway and there was nothing else to be done but to get the throttle open and get on with it. We just hammered on through the weather. It was 230 kilometres to the terminal and we were there in a little over 2 hours, non-stop.

We spent the trip through the tunnel chatting to a Dutch-Anglo couple who were into bikes so the journey was over quickly, but not quickly enough to stop us getting hot in our suits. Off the train we rode straight to one of the tunnel hotels and booked in. We were both tired even if we were still dry! It was still raining as we unpacked but some days are just like that.

South from Calais the next day we rode into a maelstrom. The semi-trailers churned the rain into a blinding storm of water that buffeted us constantly. At times I could see little through my helmet visor as the cold water seeped in and splashed into my eyes. The helmet pads soaked up the water and it found its way into my suit around the neck seal. Our gloves (the 'waterproof' model, mind you) were spongy with cold water. We didn't say much through the intercom. There wasn't much to say. I just kept the throttle open and we punched into the turbulent air, hammering our way through each knot of semis to some clean air beyond. I could feel Jo tucked in behind me trying to keep out of the blast. Every now and then I would ask her if she was OK, but she was always 'fine' no matter how wet or cold it got.

We were able to make up time on the hills where the auto-route had an extra lane for passing. With the throttle against the stop in 6th gear, the Elephant pulled like two bastards thundering passed trucks, little Citroëns and Mercs alike. We had no respect. The 430 kilometres to Orléans still took us more than seven hours but we found a hotel, food and wine without problems and set about drying our gear.

Some days are just bastards.

On our third day in the rain, we climbed onto the central plateau with altitudes up to 600 metres. The temperature plummeted. It was wet *and* cold. How good could it get? On the 540 kilometres run from Orléans to Montauban, we tried the last 200 kilometres on the back roads. Our only excuse for this was the streaker's defence: it seemed like a good idea at the time. The route took us through small villages with indifferent grip on the local roads. There were lots of those slip 'n' grip moments that bike riders find character forming. Fortunately there were no slip 'n' slip moments.

Eight more hours in the rain had left us exhausted. We found a pizza joint and splurged on a US$6 bottle of red (who said we were on a tight budget?). We dried our gear again.

Our next day was to take us over one of the passes through the Pyrenées. This didn't seem like a good idea considering the weather, so we spent some valuable sleeping time planning an alternate route around to the east and down the Mediterranean coast. In the end, however, we were just too tired to make a sensible decision and decided to sleep on it.

We awoke to find the morning of 31 October was dry. To be more precise, it wasn't raining! We checked what passes for a weather report on French TV, sized up the sky, and decided to stick to the plan and run for the mountains. We raced south on the toll road, hoping that if we went quickly the weather gods might not bother about us for a day.

The mountains rose up in front of us, white caps and all, but the roads started to dry and the rain stayed away. We wound up through the hills until they became mountains and then wound up some more. The road climbed through the snow line where it became wet, and ploughed through a 5.2-kilometre tunnel built at a time when cars and trucks were smaller. I was wearing my old RayBans for the ride up but there was no opportunity to remove them before plunging into the half-light. To make matters worse, the headlight on the Elephant was very poor. In the gloom the trucks seemed to be inches away on one side and the tunnel wall touchable on the other. I kept the bike pointing straight and relied on its suspension to soak up the pot-holes. There was no room for fancy riding! We burst out into the bright mountain light with a blast of icy air and me making a mental note to take off the sunglasses before the next 5-kilometre tunnel. The GPS put the altitude at 1683 metres. The snow had started at 800 metres.

Over the watershed, we tumbled down the mountain roads into Spain feeling pretty good about ourselves, chatting about the changed landscape on the southern side of the mountains and enjoying the winding, dry mountain road and warming air. Finally we were putting some wear on the sides of the tyres and enjoying it! The side winds on the run into Zaragosa were the strongest we had ever experienced. Probably stronger than those that had forced us to stop overnight in Yass 30 years before (many would say that no cross wind is that strong). But this minor distraction only served to heighten our anticipation of Spanish adventures.

Zaragosa was our first Spanish city and we were impressed. The city had beautiful public spaces, a lovely and lively city centre and enough tapas bars to sink a ship. We tried a couple, drank some cheap beer and a bottle of wine, and ate all manner of interesting stuff. By the time we crashed into bed we were tired but content.

We had one more day down to the coast, the Moto GP weekend and a week off in Calpe. The challenges of the preceding days had left us quietly confident in the Elephant, the gear and ourselves. We were not afraid of wet weather, cold, crazy drivers, crowded cities or mountain tunnels. It was that sort of satisfied feeling that always precedes a crisis.

At 6am on Thursday 1 November 2007 our global roaming mobile woke us from deep sleep. It was my mother to tell me that my father had died three hours earlier. We started our little computer, purchased some WiFi time from a local provider and started to reorganize our lives. By checkout time we had airfares booked from Barcelona to London and on to Sydney, some of our accommodation was sorted and we had the germ of a plan for storing the bike. We paid the toll on the *autopista* and charged out of town like one of the Spanish fighting bulls the area is famous for. We forgot about the fuel economy for a rush to Barcelona.

With the sort of timing that we only appreciate in hindsight, 1 November was a Holy Day holiday in Spain and everything was closed. CLOSED! In Barcelona we got back onto the net and prepared for the next day. We had worked out four options to store the bike starting with the local BMW dealers, followed by the local BMW club, then a self-storage locker and finally an appeal to the police to impound the bike for a few weeks. We also found the contact details for the Australian Consulate in case we needed it. We got the addresses for the two BMW dealers and did a careful reconnaissance of the routes to each. The first one was posted with a sign saying (if our Spanish could be relied on) that the business would be closed the next day, Friday, to make a 4-day weekend of it. The other was a combined car dealership and looked like it might be open on the Friday.

Back in the hotel we had dinner early (in Spain 'early' means 8pm), checked our lists of addresses and telephone numbers and tried to get some sleep. We also made sure all our gear was packed ready for a quick departure. Because of a big conference in town, we could only get one night in that hotel and would have to change pubs somewhere in the process.

Thanks to the route reconnaissance we were parked outside the BMW dealer at 8.30am. Jo stood guard on our worldly possessions while I found the *moto* part of the business and a mechanic who spoke some English and, eventually, the Moto Service Manager, Marc, who spoke a little more English. I told him the problem in a few words. Yes, that would be OK. He would service the bike and do a special check of the brakes and hold it for us until we returned in three weeks. Deal done! It was 9.15am.

We spent a few hours riding around in the traffic getting a feel for Barcelona before cruising out to the expensive airport hotel that had a room available. We repacked the side and back boxes with stuff we would leave on the bike, left our carry bags in the pub and headed back to the BMW dealer. Handing over the bike took only a few minutes. We left our helmets and jackets in Marc's locker and handed him our Moto GP tickets in appreciation of his support. He was still grinning and thanking me for the tickets when we walked out into the streets of Barcelona without the machine that had regulated our lives for the last two months. We felt a little naked.

The next two and a half days were just travel: airplanes, trains and buses. Our hasty escape plan rolled out with only a few hitches and we misplaced a day and landed in Sydney at 9pm on Monday night. From a standing start in the middle of Spain on a public holiday, we were back inside four days. Sombre and tired, but back.

Some weeks are merciless.

My father, Matthew John Hannan, escaped a life of grinding rural poverty in the Irish Republic to join the Royal Marines and fight in WWII. He served on the battleship King George V and came to Australia when she anchored in Sydney for boiler repairs. He never went back to Ireland, discharging in Sydney at the end of the war. He struggled his whole life to find his place in the New World. His business ventures failed to deliver the prosperity he wanted but through it all he married and raised a family and loved his adopted home like a native.

Dad had been sick with emphysema for a long time and, having lost part of a lung to cancer several years before, his health had deteriorated inexorably. It was clear before we left on our journey that he may not live to see our return and this was one of the many factors with which I struggled in making the decision to go. We had included in our budget a provision for one return trip home hoping that it would remain unspent. Over the year leading up to our departure I had made the trip from our Gold Coast home to see him in the Blue Mountains behind Sydney several times. On each visit I was surprised at his deterioration but even the relentless march of his illness had a positive benefit.

These circumstances gave me an opportunity to talk to him in a far more personal way that I had ever managed before. I don't recall the exact words that I used on our last visit, but the sense of what I tried to say was that he had been a good man and had led a good life and that he was leaving behind a legacy of a family that was thriving in this new land. He thanked me for saying this, and with tears in his eyes told me he knew it was OK to die now.

After the funeral, I stayed on to help with the paperwork for a week while Jo took the opportunity to visit her own elderly mother in Sydney. We had booked our return tickets at the same time as we booked the inward journey so we had a fixed departure date to hurry our efforts and although there was still much to be done, we flew out on 20 November bound for London and Barcelona. We arrived on the night of 21 November, missing two days sleep, but otherwise intact. A late night dinner of local sausage and white beans and a few hours sleep reset the gyros for Spain.

On the morning of 22 November we walked to the BMW dealer

and found the Elephant moping around the back of the workshop, fraternising with shiny new bikes whose owners washed them and probably treated them very well indeed; no place for our beast of burden. We thanked Marc for looking after our bike and gear for three weeks, paid our bill and got the bike back to our hotel to start getting it ready for the next leg of our journey. The brakes, we were told, had tested OK.

During our unexpected detour, I had made up two additional storage tubes to increase the volume of storage for our cold weather gear. One of the problems had been that we needed to carry gear for very cold weather, but we didn't need to use it all the time. The cold weather stuff wasn't heavy, but it was bulky and we simply didn't have sufficient lockable storage.

Each of the two kits consisted of a 150 mm storage tube with a watertight screw-on end and all of the hardware needed to fix it under one of the side boxes. We also brought back a small hand drill and drill bit to use for fixing and the necessary sealants and packing foam to make it a watertight and secure job.

The remainder of our first day and well into the evening was spent fitting up the storage kits to the side boxes. When the job was finally done and all of the gear loaded, we were both too tired to go out for a meal and collapsed into bed hoping to catch up on some sleep. Unfortunately, the hotel was old and thin walled. The noise from the street was annoying but the noise when the gentleman in the next room took a Spanish folk dancing lesson from a professional instructor was enough to wake the dead. It was certainly enough to wake us!

We had a grumpy breakfast and headed out of Barcelona at 10.30am on the morning of 21 November after giving Kylie (the GPS) Valencia as our first destination. It was about then that the day started to go wrong. Jo reckons it was my fault. She claims that after not speaking to *her* for three weeks I should not have re-started our relationship by saying 'come on you old tart, get your sorry arse into gear and let's get this rock show moving!' Whatever the cause, Kylie gave us clear and unambiguous directions that took us west and inland onto the central plateau rather than straight south down the coast to Valencia. I only noticed there was something wrong when the road kept climbing and when I checked the altitude we were at 760 metres and my hands were numb with the cold. We stopped for coffee, warm clothes and a long hard look at the map. I punched Kylie's buttons firmly and set a course straight back to the coast. It was 2pm by the time we were back on the coastal road only 100 kilometres from our start.

For the next day we headed south staying off the *autopista* and rolling along on the minor roads through towns and villages, across endless plains of orange orchards and around huge sprawling industrial towns with every kind of factory. Every now and then our minor road crossed under the *autopista*, with its traffic flashing by, but we were happy weaving our way through Spaniards going about their daily business.

Every few kilometres in the rural areas a young lady dressed in the traditional costume of Spanish folk dancing instructors sat by the road on a plastic chair waiting for students from among the long distance truck drivers and tourists who mill along the coastal strip. At least, that is how it was explained to me.

Our destination was the town of Calpe which is a large tourist centre catering to Germans and Britons seeking a place in the sun. Off season, with the cold wind whipping whitecaps onto the normally calm Mediterranean, it had a seedy and unhurried charm. Calpe is not the sort of town that we usually frequent but we had booked several days' accommodation there to cover us for the Valencia Moto GP. The hotel had kindly agreed to allow us to transfer our pre-paid booking when we missed the original dates. Regardless of our reason for being there, we were pleased to have a few days in a (heated) apartment to get ourselves settled again.

Our digs were comfortable, off-season-cheap, and equipped with a good kitchen so we could keep eating costs down. As a consequence, it was an easy decision to extend our stay by two days (to six) to catch up on some R&R. At least that was the plan! We started to stride around the area, getting some of the exercise we had missed over the last few weeks, and then decided to climb the limestone rock (Peñon de Ifach) that formed a headland at the end of our beach.

Rising 332 metres straight out of the sea, it dominated the village below. The headland had been a national park for many years and had well-established tracks up the sides. It was not, however, an easy climb and took us about an hour to scramble to the top where we had a panoramic view of the surrounding countryside. Although the wildlife service claimed there were numerous critters on the mountain, including two types of snakes, we only found the seabirds waiting to greet us. Looking up and down the coast we were startled to see a carpet of villas covering every bit of land with a southern aspect and sea view. These were generally owned by foreigners who used them to escape the northern winters or to retire in the sun. The consequence of the foreign invasion was that the Spanishness of the place had been considerably diluted. Since we had come to Valencia to see Valencians, this didn't seem like the best part of the province to be in.

An upside to the northern invasion were the few German bakeries that had appeared around the town. We were able to buy some excellent German bread that was a pleasant change from the sameness of French, Spanish and English bread. Not that I am complaining about the fresh baguette mind you, but some dark bread with real substance that lasts more than four hours is also good.

Apart from the great view, the climb to the top of the mountain had other consequences. For Jo, it aggravated a back strain she had carried for some time after a disagreement with my mother's lawnmower. For me it aggravated a long-standing arthritic complaint in my left foot. Jo agreed to take it easy for a while and to leave the 'lifting heavy things stuff' to me, but this proved to be more easily said than done. For my part, I have always been one to go the drugs early so I found a local doctor to get some medication.

The doctor, an attractive woman in her mid-fifties, had been trained in Argentina. She spoke fluent German and good English but wandered past the waiting room to say hello to her new patient with a cigarette hanging out of her mouth. She took one look at the offending foot and gave what I knew to be the correct diagnosis. She then announced that she had had the same complaint since she was 10 years old and proceeded to pull up her shirt to show where she had a kidney removed because the complaint had been misdiagnosed and mismanaged. She then dragged down a lever arch binder full of articles and pictures on what turned out to be her pet disease!

In short order, what followed was an anti-inflammatory injection, a blood test and prescriptions for a slack-handful of drugs and a lot of advice that was hastily scribbled into the travel journal. By the time I left the surgery the injection had kicked in and I walked the two kilometres back to the pub at the usual brisk pace and without discomfort. Within a couple of days I could operate the gear change on the Elephant and we were ready to go.

We bolted out of Calpe early on the morning of 29 November happy to escape in one piece (each) for the run over to Granada, which was a little over 400 kilometres away, on the excellent Spanish A roads. With a short stop for lunch in a park in Lorca, we were into Granada town by mid-afternoon. On the way, a simple fact of Spanish geography finally dawned on us. Spain, it turns out, has the second highest average altitude in Europe after Switzerland. As soon as we left the narrow coastal strip we started climbing, eventually reaching 1360 metres at the highest point on the central range. This was accompanied by the obvious low temperatures. After the central range, Granada itself was perched above the plain (La Vega) at a pleasant 685 metres; about the same altitude as Canberra.

Without a map of the city, we relied entirely on Kylie to get us into the centre and to find a pub. This proved to be a problem. The streets in the old city were narrow, satellite contact was hard to maintain and most alleys were one-way but not reflected as such in the mapping. After an hour and a half of wrestling the Elephant down narrow lanes I had had enough. Unfortunately so had the Elephant! The brake failure light started flashing on the dash and the rear brake stopped working. Now, for those who are not bike riders, the back brake doesn't do that much work while on the open road but is very important in slow speed manoeuvring, particularly with a big, heavily laden bike like the Elephant. The technique is to 'drag' the back brake at the same time as the throttle is used to stand the bike up. This allows you to maintain engine power and drive to keep the bike stable in very slow turns. On BMW bikes like the Elephant, the front and back brakes are controlled by the same ABS/servo system and if the back goes out there is every chance that the front will follow. We cut our losses and headed back to the outskirts of town, found a chain motel, beer and food and licked our wounds.

On Saturday morning we put on our determined faces and plunged back into town, still without back brakes. Granada is not a very big place, so when we report that it took 90 minutes to find the tourist office and a further 90 minutes to find the first pub on our list, you will understand that the search wasn't a highpoint of our day. Halfway through this test of patience we were pulled over by the police for the first time on this trip. Two officers, mounted on gleaming white Honda Transalps, blocked our way at the end of an alley and demanded to know why we were going the wrong way down a one-way street.

'Kylie made me do it,' I said while pointing to the GPS. I don't think the joke translated very well to Spanish. The real reason; that there is no rhyme or reason to the one-way streets, went unsaid. We got a stern talking to and were allowed to go on our way.

The pub we found wasn't great, but it was clean and we had managed to park the bike within 150 metres. We left Elephant to sulk over the broken brakes and set out to find out what Granadans do on a weekend.

We spent Saturday and Sunday walking the old city, wandering the narrow lanes and taking the compulsory tour of the Alhambra Palace. Despite its press, the Alhambra was a little disappointing. While the design was admirably adapted to the hot Spanish summers, it would have been a damned cold place in winter and the quality of the workmanship in its construction was not up to the best contemporary standards.

The city does have plenty of history though. The Church of

Saint Domingo was the place where the Court of the Inquisition celebrated its festivities. However, on the Sunday morning we visited all they could organise was a christening without an Inquisitor in sight. We sat in the sun on a bench in the square in front and surveyed the crumbling facade of the old church. It was rundown and poorly maintained and was like hundreds of other near derelict churches we had seen across Spain. Under the long Franco reign, the church had supported, and had been supported by, the state. The new democratic Spain, however, was showing that it has a deeply secular heart. Deprived of congregations and money, many beautiful churches were boarded up for public safety, too poor to carry out the repairs that would stop their rotting stonework crashing down on the faithful. Jo thought the boarded-up churches looked sad and neglected but I didn't take that view. They had been able to prosper under the patronage of a repressive regime and now they needed to find relevance by their own merit.

All of this tourist stuff, however, just got us to Monday morning and sorting out the brake problem. The BMW dealer was about 1.5 kilometres away and I got the bike over there at about 8am (and 4°C). At reception they found a mechanic who spoke a little English and agreed to look at it straight away. I went for coffee and breakfast and returned two hours later. By this time the Elephant was missing some parts and looked a little miserable. Then came the bad news. The ABS/servo unit was stuffed and would have to be replaced. A new one could be sent from Madrid overnight at a cost of €1600 for the part.

I pointed out that as far as I was concerned, the bike still had two months of warranty left. The Service Manager demurred and what followed was one of those short brutal conversations that service managers must hate. Documents were photocopied and sent to BMW and after a short delay it was agreed that the bike was indeed still under warranty, there would be no charge and it would be ready the next afternoon.

I started the walk back to the hotel full of foreboding and thinking that if this unit packed it in somewhere in North Africa, with or without warranty, it would be a disaster. However, by the time I was back at the pub I had a plan. If the ABS/servo unit broke again, then any brake shop could rig a by-pass for both the front and rear systems. Lever pressures would be high without servo assistance, but the bike would stop and I would build up some hand muscles. If the lever pressure was too high, I could always replace the BMW master cylinder with one from a non-servo bike and plumb it straight to the callipers. Team Elephant, I decided, wasn't going to be beaten that easily.

When I got back to our digs, Jo was a little surprised that I wasn't more depressed by the bad news and didn't seem quite so sanguine about my plan for a fix should it occur again.

'Trust me,' I said.

'I did once,' she responded. 'That's how we ended up with two children.'

So, with the relentless approach of the winter cold, we spent several days in Granada waiting for parts from Madrid with a map of Morocco spread out across the bed studying the high mountain passes and the edges of the Sahara. In the meantime we started to get a feel for the rhythm of Spanish life. It was becoming perfectly normal to eat chocolate covered donuts for breakfast, have a beer and tapas anytime and sit down to dinner at 10pm. Wonderful sounding words like 'Hombre', 'Naranja' or 'Amigo' started to roll deliciously off the tongue and the Spanish love of life started to creep into our bones.

I went back to pick up the Elephant at 3.50pm after two days and found the workshop deserted. Normally, we would take this to mean that the surf was up and everyone has knocked off early. In Spain it simply meant that no one was back from lunch yet. At 3.57pm they poured in with a roar of bikes and cars and flooded the workshops and offices with noise and movement. The dealership was open until 8pm each day. Elephant was waiting, still needing a wash, but looking good for a ride. I thanked the service manager, took a quick photograph and got going before anything else could break.

By the end of November, Granada was just too cold for us. We had only extended our stay because of the breakdown, so we packed and prepared for a cold ride. There had to be somewhere warm in Spain and our mission had become to find it. We headed west towards Cadiz and the coast and made great time flying up through the mountain passes and across endless plains of olive trees.

Our destination was the town of Jerez de la Frontera. It was not on the usual tourist short list but was of interest to us as the home of the world sherry industry and all of the large sherry houses (called Bodegas). The town had about 185,000 inhabitants; lots of rich folk thanks to the sherry industry, but high unemployment because the sherry industry was the only industry of size. It was a modern, practical sort of place that was already starting to ruffle itself up for the Christmas holiday. Our decision to stay there for four days was less related to the town's attractions and more to the fact that Thursday 6 December and Saturday 8 December were both public holidays, and, as we found with All Saints' Day in Barcelona, the locals were sure to take the Friday off and make it a four-day weekend. We decided the best option was not to be looking for food and lodgings over the break. We found lots of tourists in town on the public holiday, but the vast majority were Spanish discovering their own country. The English and Germans had come in the summer.

The town had a considerable English influence and several of the bodegas were English owned. The investment in Jerez dated back to the 17th Century but really took off in the 19th Century when the English army brought back a taste for sherry after the Napoleonic war.

We decided to visit the Gonzalez Byass Bodega and found that we were the only starters for the English language tour. Jo thought this was fair compensation for having ridden to Jerez on a bike in the winter. The tour guide, Andrea, was from Slovakia, spoke excellent English and Spanish and was informative company for the 90-minute tour. She looked a million dollars in her smart corporate overcoat too, with us looking dowdy in the same old riding gear.

After the stinginess of the French, we almost laughed out loud when we were given a table in the tasting room and had an un-opened bottle plonked down with the instruction to try this one first (a sweeter one would follow). We were not sure how the Spaniards defined 'tasting', but this was more like 'drinking' where we came from. We made a good start on the chilled Palomino Fino and rolled out with a rosy glow after two hours, in need of a siesta but pleased that we had spent our €18 well.

On our final day in Jerez we decided to visit the National Flamenco Museum. Unfortunately we made the mistake of visiting on another Feast Day (Immaculate Conception) only to find that it was closed. Normally we would have been surprised that a museum was closed during a public holiday, but since the times for opening and closing of all manner of things had completely eluded us during our month in Spain, we shrugged our shoulders and went looking for a tapas bar instead.

In a way the closed museum was emblematic of our time here: we turned up, but it was closed. The day we left Jerez for the short ride to the coastal port of Algeciras and a boat to Morocco, we planned to have breakfast at a cosy café just around the corner from the hotel. We packed the bike and rode around to find the place closed and a couple of locals peering in and checking their watches. Spain can be like that. We didn't stop to investigate but kept riding south with me humming an old Dylan song inside my helmet: *Spanish is the Loving Tongue*. The lyrics were a little hazey, but the pretty tune was strong and melodic and I started to sing out loud...

Tangier

Asilah

Rabat

Casablanca

El-Jadida

. Fes

Oualidia

Morocco

Essaouira

Marrakech

Agadir

Algeria

Western Sahara

5

Flat on Our Backs in Morocco

By early December the short, cold winter days were just too much for a pair of misplaced Queenslanders so as soon as we were clear of Spanish holidays we packed and slipped away from Jerez in the early morning fog. A few hours later in Algeciras we took a 10th floor hotel room with a view over the busy port and across to Gibraltar. It was already a few degrees warmer at sea level. There are few things finer than a room overlooking a port. The constant movement of ships and the general hubbub and colour on the docks are always exciting. Waiting for our departure to a new country on a new continent they were doubly so.

We checked all the ferry companies until we found a vessel departing at 8am the next morning, purchased tickets for ourselves and the Elephant, then wandered the city to see what mischief we could find. Alas, with the countdown to Christmas, the best we could do was a local choir singing Spanish Christmas carols in the plaza so we adjourned back to the pub to watch the port and check our paperwork.

At 7am on 10 December, we rode down to the docks, were waved through customs and immigration and rode onto our ship. By 8am we were underway and it was *Adios* Spain. Three hours later we landed in Tangiers: *Ssalamu 'lekum Maroc* (roughly translated: 'How do you do, Morocco').

We were not entirely new to the way things are done in this part of the world so, as soon as the ferry docked, we hustled the Elephant into the melée around the Border Police post. We paid a generous 'tip' to get to the front of the queue and have the paperwork for the bike sorted, and rolled out onto the streets of Tangier in about 15 minutes. A quick stop to get fuel and change some money took only a few minutes more, then we were off up the hill and into the thick of the Tangier traffic. Just like in other parts of North Africa and the Middle East where we have travelled, it is chaos in slow motion: folks wander across the road without any regulation, cars and trucks drift across 'lanes' and no-one ever looks at their rear view mirrors. The unwritten rule is always 'if I am in front, I have right of way'. The bikes here are mostly tiny mopeds and the cars are small and low-powered so it all has a surreal feel for us. There is nothing of the lethal intensity of our own traffic with many more vehicles and ballistic speeds. Best of all, it happens with good humour and the traffic manages to flow despite the best efforts of everyone. We bustled through Tangier and found the Atlantic coast road heading south for the little village of Asilah. Tangier could wait until we were on our way out of Morocco.

Big motorbikes were fairly rare in this part of the world especially after bike-mad Spain. People stared openly as we zoomed past and, when we stopped, asked all of the standard questions: how big, how heavy, how fast? To which the answers were: too big, too heavy and not bloody fast enough!

Asilah was a very pretty town of blue and white houses clustered on a small headland jutting into the Atlantic. It was full of tourists in the summer, but almost deserted when we visited. An overnight there allowed us to get our bearings in the new country. We had a couple of good meals, a good night's sleep and then headed south again to Rabat, the capital city. Our route took us along the rural roads and away from the freeway that links Tangier with the great cities of the south and interior. We crossed inland over the vast plains of the Ouerra River Valley.

This area is many times larger than the Darling Downs and the plains of alluvial topsoil rolled out in a patchwork of brown and green in a vast display of natural wealth. The river and a tributary are dammed up-stream and there is an extensive irrigation system providing water for agriculture. The elevated aqueducts marched backwards and forwards across the valley in dull concrete-grey uniform steps. There were some substantial agricultural enterprises fed by the channelled water, with good levels of mechanisation and they looked well run and prosperous. But we did notice sections of the aqueducts that were in disrepair and there was plenty of evidence of poor maintenance.

Although the large holdings were impressive, the greatest area of this fertile plain was given over to small farmers ploughing a few acres with wooden framed ploughs and donkeys. In many cases we saw lucerne being mown by hand; hard work for sure, but not profitable work. As we travelled south over the next week we were struck again and again by the richness of the land, but for every commercial enterprise likely to generate real wealth for the economy, there was 10 times the area given over to small cropping at almost subsistence level. We learned that, by law, the Moroccan Government was required to find employment for all and that any widespread reform of agriculture would throw a substantial number of agricultural workers out of employment. There are, of course, lots of political and social reasons that the government of a developing nation might want to maintain stability and employment. None of them, however, make much economic sense and the ability of governments to subvert the ideals of a constitution for the enrichment of the political elites is always boundless.

Rabat was a modern city of about 1.8 million souls. As befits a capital, it had wide boulevards with modern cafés, a cosmopolitan population, and a sophisticated feel. We spend three nights there to get a feel for modern Morocco and found it a place of contrasts with many new, often western influences mixed with traditional Moroccan practice. The locals blended the old with the new more seamlessly than we expected. The old walled city, or *medina*, was also a surprise. It was much more vibrant and less geared to the tourist than we had expected. The narrow lanes were brilliant with colour and life, the spice sellers presided over an empire of a thousand pungent lands, and the hustle of trading filled the air with the constant cry for trade.

The old *kasbah*, or administrative centre, had been rebuilt and smartened up for the tourists but even here the crush was of locals going about their business and outsiders were hard to find. Below the *kasbah*, on a tiny fringe of yellow sand, we found the Rabat Surf Club and some hardy souls prepared to paddle their boards out into the early-winter Atlantic during the long midday break of a working day.

On our last day in Rabat we sought out the English language bookshop to replenish our reading supplies. The tiny shop was jam-packed with second-hand and new books. Stacked shelves stretched from floor to ceiling on all walls and thousands more titles were piled high on tables that almost filled the remaining space. We found we could just squeeze between the book-mountains by turning sideways and being careful. We searched through the stacks looking for books we would both read as we could only carry a few. Although there is plenty of overlap in our tastes, suitable books were often hard to to find as the ex-pat bookshops never seemed to have our literary common ground covered. Fortunately this was a better than average bookshop and we quickly found four new books and could have purchased a dozen more had there been a place to carry them. As we were about to leave, we struck up a conversation with another customer, a Moroccan named Khalid Ammani. Khalid was an English language teacher working at a number of schools. His English was excellent and, like all Moroccans, he was a great conversationalist. Khalid invited us for coffee and then to join him with his Intermediate English class at a nearby language institute that evening. Not having anything planned (the story of our lives) we were pleased to accept.

Khalid's class was an adult education group. There were two blokes and about a dozen women, and they ranged in age from a 16 year old to several in their thirties. They were well educated and bright and, like adult education students everywhere, very clear about why they were studying. We spent about 90 minutes talking about ourselves and our travels with the Elephant and asking them about Morocco. The word 'codger' came up in discussion about our ages and it is such a great word to roll around the tongue, that I wrote it on the board and recommended it for use in polite company. For us, the visit was a delight. We left reassured that if these young folk were the future of Morocco, there would be plenty of good things happening here.

Through these first few days, Jo and I had been settling down to Moroccan food. The Spanish had been quite structured in their feeding arrangements; although you could get beer and tapas anytime, and there was plenty of good street food, the Spanish were not generally snackers. Moroccan eating arrangements were more familiar to us, with little formality around meal times and plenty of snacking going on anytime. We had worked out that having food that was tasty, affordable and readily available was essential for our comfort on the road, and Morocco got a gold star in this respect.

With the cool winter weather we especially appreciated the *tajines*. We had eaten these before but here, in the home of the *tajine*, they reach another level of wholesome tastiness. One evening Jo curled up in bed and complained that she felt uncomfortably full. I pointed out that the fact that she eaten a *tajine* for lunch and another for dinner may have had something to do with her condition. We were finally eating too well!

In Rabat we also saw our first example of Moroccan political dissent. While enjoying coffee with Khalid in a sidewalk café across from the National Parliament, demonstrators gathered in the street and started marching up and down and chanting slogans. They were academics and educated professionals who were protesting for more government jobs. Khalid explained that these well-educated folk felt that more of their number should be on the government payroll. A life outside the public sector was considered too uncertain for such highly educated folk. I mumbled something to Khalid about the need to get the talented folk into the private sector where growth and jobs could be created, and let it go at that because there are obviously impediments to private sector growth that outsiders like us could only guess at. Certainly, even as outsiders, and even so soon in our Moroccan adventure, we had seen that endemic corruption and family patronage were everywhere and we were sure we would learn more about these things later. In the meantime, we were content to drink our coffee and enjoy the show.

By the time we had arrived in Rabat we had been on the road for more than three months and constantly packing and unpacking the bike had been keeping us in good shape. In Rabat we had nine flights of stairs leading up to our room on which to get some 'codgercise' and three days of that was more than enough to encourage us to leave for Casablanca.

Casablanca was a 3-hour ride south on the back roads and a number of people had questioned the sanity of going there at all. With a population of 3.8 million it is a big city by any standards. It is a port and commercial centre with little of touristic interest and little interest in tourists.

With no GPS mapping and no paper maps except a page torn from a Lonely Planet, we ploughed straight into the centre of another new city. Within an hour we had found a comfortable room in a quiet hotel, secure parking for the bike in the workshop of a local mechanic, and omelettes for our lunch. A brisk walk around the city gave us the lay of the land and served as a reconnaissance for the way out of town on departure. Some days on the road everything falls into place just like that.

Casa (you can only use 'Casa' if you have been there) has some elegant and still beautiful administrative buildings dating from the colonial period but not much else of interest. It is noisy, smelly and fast-moving and we soon started to suspect that people only came there to make money. Nonetheless, we found a few things of interest. The old French cathedral, with its stained-glass window long since boarded up, had been turned into a general purpose hall, and the High Court, which dated from 1925 and the French colonisation, was still a beautiful and elegant building, understated and in perfect proportion.

Casablanca's main monument was the Hassan II Mosque. There were no points for guessing which king built it at a cost of nearly half a billion US dollars. It had in-slab heating, a glass section of the floor so that worshipers could see the crashing Atlantic Ocean below and a retractable roof, opening just like a football stadium. The day we visited it we avoided the underground car park and swung into the neighbouring suburb to park. We found ourselves in a pretty tough part of town where the road was thick with diesel-engine oil from the local truckers dumping the contents of their trucks' sumps into the drains. God is clearly hanging with rough company in Casa. The mosque itself was grandiose and ugly, built to excess and, by the look of it, not used much. It was, however, no more excessive than grand religious monuments everywhere. It was just newer.

After Casablanca we rolled south along the narrow coastal road waving back to the shepherd boys beside the road and stopping at El-Jadida and Oualidia. It was a lovely ride through this pleasant and fertile countryside. Along the road, forests of eucalypts had been harvested for firewood, the brown topsoil ran right to the sea and, in many cases, green pastures grew up to the edge of cliffs that dropped into the surf below. We ended our first week in Morocco enjoying the winter sun and watching the tide fill the Oualidia Lagoon. It was a pleasant outlook but it was to be the place that nearly stopped the show.

The winter weather was chasing us south and our hotel room at Oualidia was unheated and short on hot water. The first morning we decided to brave a cold shower telling each other that it was character forming. Jo, who was always more awake than me in the mornings, went first. She hadn't been at it long when I heard her cry out and ran in to see what had happened. I found her standing in the shower cubical, ankle deep in water, holding her back in obvious pain. She had slipped trying to pick up some dropped soap and wrenched her back injury. I got her to the bed and flat on her back where she spent the rest of the day. That evening she struggled to walk 25 metres to the dining room and grimaced all the way through dinner. She needed rest, anti-inflammatory drugs and painkillers but it was a week before Christmas and we were stuck in a freezing hotel room a long way from anywhere. Furthermore, our next stop was to be Essaouira where we had arranged for Mike and Sarah to join us for a week over the holiday. We waited another day and a half hoping for improvement.

The evening before our departure, Jo decided that if she could get onto the bike, then she would be OK to sit there, provided the road wasn't too rough and we didn't have to make too many stops. In the morning I helped her to dress then got the bike packed and ready to go. We found the best place for her to mount and I held the Elephant steady while she climbed onto the back, grinding her teeth but stoic as a trooper. Sometimes tough days creep up on you but we knew this one would be tough from the start.

We rolled south towards Essaouira on Thursday 20 December with Jo sitting bolt upright on the pillion and the Elephant stepping as smooth and bump free as possible. The coastal strip was heavily populated and farmed with the fertile land tilled down to the edge of a placid Atlantic. The villages were close together and we noticed that there was much greater activity in the villages than we had seen in previous days. In particular, there were many markets set up along the road with huge crowds and much excitement with lots of sheep being traded. We saw them crammed into the back of taxis, strapped onto roof racks and tied across the rumps of donkeys; all of them were complaining loudly. At first we didn't think much of this, as Thursday was generally market day before the Friday holy day, but we made a note to ask about the spike in ovine trading later and did our best to enjoy the ride. We had found an apartment in Essaouira on the internet and arrived in town to meet the owner with an hour to spare, which gave us time to have a good look around. Once again, we noticed huge crowds in the shopping areas outside the old city and pouring in and out of the city gates. By the time we were ready to take over the apartment at 3pm, the reason for all the frantic activity had become apparent: the next day, Friday 21 December, was the Festival of Sacrifice (Eid al-Adha), which leads into a long weekend during which nothing much would be open.

The apartment was in the *medina* of the old city and no vehicles were allowed into this area. We found a garage outside the walls that would store the Elephant and paid a man with a hand cart to carry our baggage. He loaded the bags and took off through the city with me and the landlord in hot pursuit and Jo left walking slowly and painfully behind.

The old city *souk* , or bazaar, was a crush of shoppers all intent on making their purchases before the three-day holiday. Fruit, vegetables, meat and spices were being touted in a cacophony so loud it was difficult to make out individual cries. Women bustled each other to wave notes at stall holders and snatch away bags of produce then push into the crowd looking for the next purchase. With the close of business looming, stall holders cried out their special prices all hoping to clear stock before the holiday.

By the time we reached the apartment, the penny had finally dropped: we had only an hour to get enough shopping done to last three days. The apartment was at the top of five flights of narrow winding stairs. After I had got Jo up and settled (flat on her back) and all our gear stowed, I felt more like a quiet lie down than a bout of close combat in the markets, but I headed dutifully back down the stairs and stepped out into the alley. At this point it started to rain.

Now in most places rain is just rain, but it doesn't rain much in Morocco and the streets are not plumbed to handle it. After an hour, many streets were like rivers, the crowd of last minute shoppers like salmon fighting against the current. I splashed along the flooded streets with the cold winter rain running down my back, stopping at stalls for fruit, vegetables, meat, harissa, preserved lemons, olives, oil and everything else I could think of that four people might need for a week when all the shops were likely to be closed.

It took three expeditions to carry home the supplies, which included 20 litres of bottled water, and each time I faced the stairs up to the apartment they looked steeper and longer. By dark I was soaked to the skin and cold, and the stores were closed. Unfortunately, the only alcohol shop (alcohol is readily available in Morocco but only from special shops or restaurants) had closed early. I had wasted a long jog to the far side of the old city and we were without a glass of wine, but this seemed to be a small defeat in scheme of things.

We celebrated our lucky circumstances with mint tea, which is a local specialty, settled into a little domesticity after living on the road for some weeks and started to enjoy cooking for ourselves and, for me at least, getting to know the town. Mike and Sarah arrived before lunch on the day after us by which time we had scrounged a bottle of 'interesting' Moroccan red wine from our landlady to toast our reunion dinner with.

Essaouira had been on the tourist map for years because of the ideal conditions for wind surfing in the wide bay to the north of the town. As a consequence, much of the old city was geared to the tourist trade with plenty of expensive backpacker accommodation inside the *medina* and a few very expensive hotels along the shore of the bay to its north. The narrow lanes were full of European visitors all searching for that perfect piece of Moroccan kitsch to drag back home with them. Most of the prices reflected the clientele and were far higher than we had seen in other towns.

On the day of our arrival, our landlady had pointed out a plain and unsigned door in a lane near our apartment. In there, she said, was the place to buy the best take-away *tajines* but we needed to put in orders by 4pm. Armed with this intelligence, Mike and I headed off to order dinner on our second night as residents.

We knocked and opened the door to find a tiny room with four people hard at work and a large wood-fired brick oven in one of the walls. The room was hot and the workers sweated as they sliced and diced the meat and vegetables for the next round of meals to go into the oven. The painted render walls had long since lost their colour and taken on the brown tinge of heat and smoke. The timber work tables were old, and knarled and shiny from a hundred years of service. The stone floors had furrows worn to guide the newcomer around a table that had stood barring entry to generations of customers. With our few words of French, we ordered two *tajines* to pick up at 6.30pm and left wondering how this little adventure would end.

By the time we returned for our meals the lanes were dark and the cool wind off the Atlantic had chilled the air. We pushed open the old wooden door and were met with a blast of warmth and the bustle of workers and other customers. Within a minute, two large pottery *tajines* were dragged steaming hot from the oven and sat in much used cardboard boxes for us. We let ourselves out into the night carrying the boxes, with the torturously wonderful smell of their bubbling contents directed straight at our noses from the steam holes in the *tajines'* lids and their bases burning our hands through the thick cardboard. We scurried along the lanes and up the five flights of narrow stairs with our pottery treasures, delivered them straight to the table, and lifted of the lids with a theatrical flourish. The air in our tiny apartment was instantly filled with the smell of comfort and family and we grinned at each other and toasted our good fortune in sweet dark-red Moroccan wine. Over the winter weeks ahead in the freezing Anti-Atlas Mountains, steaming hot *tajines* of mutton and vegetables with olives and preserved lemons would become our favourite comfort meal, but none of those later *tajines* would ever match this simple meal in Essaouira.

We had a relaxed and enjoyable Christmas break with no great touristic adventures but lots of sleeping-in and lazing about. The three of us kept Jo confined to the apartment and flat on her back for the most part. Rest and some anti-inflammatory drugs started to have a good effect as the days went by, but she remained worryingly sore and restricted.

A feature of the Festival of Sacrifice is that families slaughter a sheep. Each of the families around us killed theirs on the flat rooftop with cooking and feasting following close behind. Throughout all this, there was much shouting and a general good time had by all, except the sheep. Even the seagulls had a big day, picking clean the skins left to dry on the rooftop clothes lines.

We eventually had our Christmas dinner on Boxing Day at a modern restaurant nearby. The extra day gave Jo the best chance of being well enough to attend and allowed us to avoid the Christmas Day price spike. The food and wine were excellent with many dishes showing a modern take on traditional Moroccan cuisine and it was a wonderful finish to our week with Sarah and Mike. Jo's injury had had an interesting benefit as it stopped us going off exploring and kept us around the apartment, which gave us a chance to have some time with our new son-in-law for the first time. With the young couple in London and us on the Gold Coast, all of our previous time together had been rushed visits with much to do apart from sit and talk. On this occasion, there was no escape for the new husband! We made the most of it but too soon it was time to say goodbye. For Sarah and Mike it was off to Marrakech before returning to chilly London and for us it was back to the road. Jo managed the walk back across the *medina* and we found the Elephant where we had left it in a local garage. I suspected that it had been cross breeding with mopeds. The luggage was back on the bike and by 10.30am, 27 December, we were 'back at the office'.

Jo found that sitting upright in the pillion seat wasn't too uncomfortable provided I kept the ride smooth and, as it turned out, this wasn't difficult. Still, we decided to go only as far as the town of Agadir a few hours south and to allow more time for recuperation. The ride down the coast road was a delightful wind through the foothills of the High Atlas where they swept down to the sea. The surface was no worse than that on many of our South East Queensland roads and the scenery was spectacular. The beaches stretched long and white into the southern distance with the crashing Atlantic surf framing a cloudless crystal blue sky.

At first sight Agadir surprised us. It had wide boulevards,

modern buildings and a broad strip of resort hotels clustered along the waterfront. What it lacked, however, was an old quarter reflecting the city's foundations as a Portuguese trading post in the 16th Century. When we asked about this, we were told that the city had been destroyed by an earthquake in 1960 and had been rebuilt. This story interested us, so we set out to find out about this catastrophe.

We were surprised to find how little of the pre-1960 city remains. The old Berber *kasbah*, located on top of a hill overlooking the new town, has been bulldozed flat and even areas of apparent significance, such the site where victims of the quake were buried in a mass grave, are largely unmarked and neglected. The small Earthquake Museum had a few interesting photos from the city's heyday as a French beach resort in the 1930s but there was little else to show for 400 years of settlement.

A chance meeting with a German Mathematics teacher and Morocco-enthusiast named Bernd Laube filled in some of the detail. According to Bernd, Agadir sits over a fault line at the foot of the High Atlas Mountains on about 1000 metres of unstable sedimentary deposits. The earthquake measured 7 on the old Richter scale and happened at 12.43am on 29 February 1960. The tremor lasted only 15 seconds but in this time the buildings of the old and new towns simply collapsed on their occupants. 15,000 people died in seconds and another 12,000 were injured. Among the old buildings of the *kasbah*, all but one thousand of the inhabitants perished in the initial seconds.

International aid was sent by the US (US Army engineers and equipment in particular), the French, Spanish and other European nations. The Americans levelled the ruins to reduce the risk of further casualties and a massive evacuation of 35,000 survivors dispersed the memory of the night.

After such a disaster, the rebuilding of Agadir was spectacular. The government insisted on a new building code, which would provide better protection from inevitable future quakes, and selected the Bauhaus, or Post Modern architectural style as this best reflected traditional housing and made best use of the three-story limit imposed by the reconstruction authority. As a result, the city has many streets with beautifully integrated Post Modern buildings. A coat of paint and even some of the poorer areas would look a treat.

While standing on the wall of the old *kasbah* pondering what had happened to the people who lived there for 500 years and then didn't, we were looking straight down on the port and were amazed by the size of the trawler fleet docked there. Several hundred large trawlers were tied up in matching sets at company docks. There were also hundreds of intermediate trawlers crowded into another area and the small open coastal dinghies were crowded into several other areas.

Being both idle and curious, there was nothing else for it but to clamber onto the Elephant, convince the port security that we had bone fide business and go and have a look for ourselves. What we found in Agadir was the world's biggest sardine fishing fleet and a mad scramble of activity. There were purposeful crushes of people unloading catches, loading ice and victuals, and there were pungent boxes of sardines everywhere. The din of human endeavour on the docks was matched by a constant screech from the circling mass of seagulls looking for easy pickings. After wandering around and taking an interest in the sardine business for a while, the only sensible response was to find a dockside restaurant and order up a plate of fresh grilled sardines and a beer for lunch.

It was during our stay in Agadir that the registration of the Elephant expired. Our solution to this was to pay the renewal over the net and have the label recovered from our redirected mail by Jo's sister Pauline. The replacement label was then scanned and emailed through to us along with the registration paper itself. At a photographic shop I had the scan printed to scale on photographic paper, trimmed the image and had it laminated. The completed facsimile was then fitted to the label holder and was so good I left it there until renewal time.

We had found a good hotel at a reasonable price with secure parking for the Elephant so we stayed on in Agadir until Jo's back was in fair shape for travel. Each day we walked a little further to give her some exercise. A few days we overdid it and had a set back, but her improvement was steady. Once she was walking three or four kilometres we knew our medical crisis had been averted and it was time to go. We finished our stay at Agadir with a New Year's Eve dinner and a bottle of Moroccan wine followed by a walk along the crowded waterfront for an ice cream. It was 34 years since the New Year's Eve we had met in Sydney and I had given Jo her first pillion ride on a bike. A lot had changed in the intervening years, but not so much as you might think.

6

Into the Moroccan Heartland

Every parking space in any big town in Morocco was controlled by a parking warden who made his meagre living by organising the parking and guarding your car or bike. I paid the guard in Agadir well to keep our Elephant safe and also had him give it a New Year's Eve wash. This was the first since leaving home. For reasons that will become obvious shortly, his effort was wasted.

On New Year's Day we rode inland from Agadir and into the mountains. Morocco is defined by its mountains. The Riff Mountains press hard against the Mediterranean in the north. The Anti-Atlas Mountains slash across the country and isolate the arid south. The Middle Atlas and mighty Atlas Mountains form a defining backbone driving from the northeast down to tumble into the sea at Agadir on the Atlantic coast. Other lesser ranges such as the Sahro ensure that almost every scene is framed by mountains. Bike riders love mountains because mountains have mountain roads!

An hour after leaving Agadir we had crossed the fertile Souss Valley and were heading into the foothills of the Anti-Atlas. The road wound up into hills that were heavily terraced to use every available piece of fertile land. In stark contrast to those on the fertile plains below, the hill farmers eked out an existence on small plots and poor soils. On the narrow terraces, all cultivation was by hand or a simple wooden plough pulled by a donkey. The villages were desperately poor and bleak, exposed to the bitter winter winds coursing down the mountain valleys.

Although the road surface was often treacherous, with gravel on almost every corner, the riding was a pleasure. There were stunning sights at every turn that kept us interested and kept drawing my eyes away from the challenge of the road. As we climbed higher through the valleys we found many *kasbah*s. Some were ancient and crumbling back to the earth. Others were still in use. All were spectacularly sited in commanding hilltop positions.

On days like this we felt the freedom of the road as a real and powerful force in our lives. The idea of being out on the road, free to go in any direction, with no deadline or agenda, had always been a romantic notion and a little adolescent and silly. A day of riding in the Moroccan mountains, even on a cold day, was enough to make us feel like we were teenagers again, off on a road trip when everything was new and exciting.

An overnight stop in the hill town of Tafraoute reintroduced us to chilly mountain weather but after a great day's riding in the foothills, we were looking forward to pressing on. From Tafraoute, we climbed north east into the Anti-Atlas Mountains along an exhilarating black snake of a road towards the mountain village of Igherm. As we climbed higher the villages clinging to the rugged hills were smaller and spread further apart. Each one was clustered around a small plot of flat fertile land where the alluvial topsoil had settled in the ravines and small valleys. While the pockets of soil were rich, there was little flat land and very little water. These villagers literally scratched out a living.

We rode on through the village of Igherm and turned south-east towards Tata through mountain valleys. We had heard that these mountains were spectacular and, like every visitor, we had heard the list of major feature films shot in the area to take advantage of the scenery, but nothing prepared us for the reality. The Anti-Atlas Mountains loom like huge skeletons stripped of vegetation and soil, all backbone and ribs, with extraordinary colours reflected from weathered minerals. The exposed and weathered hills had such a skeletal texture they looked like the massive carcasses of prehistoric creatures in shimmering metallic blues and greens.

Each corner would bring another gasp and each crest another stop for a photo. Each photo stop would leave us frustrated because our tiny pocket digital camera lacked the capacity to capture the size and majesty of this land. In the end, no camera could record the feeling of this tortured land filling the whole of our vision, framed by an achingly perfect blue sky.

The road snaked down the valley and we were exhilarated by the ride. At our overnight stop at Tata we were in great spirits. We ate a hearty Berber meal at a rambling hotel that was full of 'expeditioners' heading into or out of the deserts of the south.

These folk paid a lot of money to be squeezed into a Landrover or Landcruiser and driven into the small patch of sand that Morocco calls a desert (it wouldn't qualify in most places) where they stay at a Berber Camp before returning to the comfort of the Tata hotel. Jo and I had done our 'sleeping under the stars in the desert' stuff and, frankly, the Moroccans didn't have enough desert to impress us. We were much more interested in the mountains.

If we hadn't been so excited by the past two days of amazing riding, we might have checked the weather report and our maps more closely before making our next decision. With the sort of blissful ignorance that always precedes a beating, we decided to go north into the mountains again and into the face of a rising storm.

It would be nice to report that we were intentionally heading for the village of Taliouine, which is the centre of saffron production, but this wasn't the case. We had simply taken the wrong road out of Tata; one that wound back into the mountains to revisit the village of Igherm, this time by a different, higher mountain pass. Jo still maintains that she was responsible for this error but by this time in our journey we had stopped ascribing blame for navigational errors. In navigational matters it was better to accept that the team cocked it up.

As we rumbled up through the hills the weather closed in quickly and we found ourselves climbing through the cloud base on a treacherously slippery switchback mountain road. It started to rain and didn't stop for the remainder of the day. Although I was starting to feel comfortable on the bike by now, slow speed switchback corners would always be a problem. The Elephant required a lot of power to keep it up in corners and had a tendency to fall into a turn if I was limp-wristed with it. On a greasy road this could be a problem.

We stopped at a village café for hot coffee, and to put on more warm clothes and our outer waterproof suits (and to provide much entertainment for the locals) then pressed on through the mountains covering 45 kilometres without getting out of third gear. It was a painfully slow and tortured ride and, above the cloud line with visibility limited to a few hundred metres, there was not much to see. A few cars passed us on the road, their drivers hunched tensely over the wheel, but this was a day for staying indoors and huddling around the fire.

It was still raining when we arrived at Taliouine so we elected to leave the saffron cooperative to its own devices, find an omelette for lunch and retire to a warm, dry hotel room. The omelette we found, the warmth was a little harder to come by. The available hotel was run-down and cold. We were finding out that Moroccans didn't have much in the way of heating in their homes or hotels. It was simply too expensive. People just put on more clothing and put up with the cold. That night a German family staying at the same hotel came to dinner each with a blanket from their room to keep warm in the icy dining room. We solved the problem by eating dinner in our riding suits then snuggled into bed under as many covers as we could find.

If the Taliouine hotel had been warmer, we might have snuggled in with a novel and waited out the rain. As it was, this seemed like a second best option, so the next morning on went the nylon suits and we rolled the Elephant out onto the road. We climbed across a high mountain valley and by lunch we had reached the village of Agdz at the top of the Drãa Valley and, much to our surprise, found that we had left the rain behind.

For no particular reason, we decided to run down the valley all the way to the Sahara. We pumped in a full tank of fuel and enjoyed a pot of mint tea then turned south towards the desert. The road dropped down through a wide fertile valley and as we lost altitude we picked up temperature quickly. The road improved and the number of vehicles increased. We picked up speed and charged south out of the mountains. The fact that we were out of the hills and out of our rain suits, however, did not put us on easy street. The wind that had brought rain and snow to the mountains blew itself out across the desert creating a sand storm that limited visibility to less than 100 metres. We had never been in a sand storm on a bike before and life became difficult in new and interesting ways. We kept our helmet visors down to keep out as much dust as possible but they became coated with dust inside and out. To get them clean and return some visibility, we were forced to stop and wipe down the inside of the visors every twenty minutes or so. The fine dust got in everywhere and we kept all of the vents on our suits closed up to keep it out. Unfortunately this also kept out the cooling air with obvious consequences.

By the time we got to The Palmeraie Hotel at Zagora we were keen to get out of the sand-blast and get ourselves and the bike indoors. Like many older hotels, The Palmeraie was happy for me to park the Elephant in its foyer. The Palmeraie was also like other old hotels in other ways. The windows didn't seal and our room was covered with a film of gritty dust. When the gusts of wind hit our second story room, the windows shook and banged as though they were about to be blown in and the dust was so thick in the air in the poorly-lit hallways that it hampered visibility. Not that any of this was too much of a problem for us. We had Elephant secured and an acceptably comfortable room, and we managed to find a cold beer and some very tasty food. In our simple world-view, things were just fine.

Having come this far south, we figured we may as well go to the end of the road to the old caravan town of M'Hamid. When the wind subsided and the dust settled the following day, we headed south down the river valley. The weather looked good, we felt good and the Elephant had no complaints. The Drãa is Morocco's largest river and its valley was broad and dry with a thin line of green marking out the watercourse. A little further south from Zagora, the river simply disappeared into the desert sands only to reappear and find its way into the Atlantic just north of Tan Tan. The ride down was pleasant enough, although there was a constant stream of Landcruisers heading in the opposite direction being flogged along by maniacal looking fellows in traditional Berber rig who seemed to be in a desperate hurry to get somewhere. The poor tourists, who had paid good money for this experience, sat crammed into the other six seats looking grim-faced and worried. From what we saw in Morocco, it seemed to be mandatory to scare the life out of the paying customers on the roads as part of the experience.

We hadn't even brought the Elephant to a stop in M'Hamid when we were surrounded by touts offering guides into the desert, Berber camp-experiences and jeeps to take our luggage. We could see them coming towards us from all over the dusty central square before we had even switched off the ignition. So we didn't switch off. We just waved a cheery goodbye and headed out of town to find the desert ourselves. After all, how hard could it be to find the Sahara?

This, above all else, was the wonder of being a truly independent traveller without an itinerary. We simply didn't have to go anywhere we didn't want to go or stay anyplace we didn't want to stay and standing around in a tourist trap being pestered by touts certainly fell into this second category. Besides, the Sahara was there waiting for us. We rode a few kilometres out of town and picked up a track heading west into the hills, we turned down it and rode over the first line of dunes and there it was, stretching out before us: the desert. The Elephant was handling the sandy tracks well and the occasional camel that passed our way gave us a wide berth (it's well known that camels don't like elephants) so we pressed on until we found a lone tree and little shade where we could boil the billy and have some lunch.

I stopped the bike on the track and Jo hunted around to find something solid to put under the sidestand to stop it sinking in the soft earth. We had just got this chore done when, almost on cue, a bunch of Berbers turned up in a beat-up old Renault R4 and offered to take us to their desert camp for a sleep-over. The poor little car was overloaded with people and stores bulging out of every opening. We groaned and sent them packing with a few sharp words. They took the rejection in good humour, piled back into the car and headed west down the track. Fifty metres further on the poor little car sank into the sand, its wheels spinning uselessly, its belly grounded.

We had been told many times since we arrived in Morocco that these folk were the desert experts so I considered for a moment taking the Elephant over and pulling them out just for the sheer hoot of being able to do it. But the damage it may have done to the Elephant's clutch just wasn't worth the bragging rights so we packed up and left them to it! We could stop anywhere for lunch after all.

Having had quite enough desert experiences for one day, and with the weather and road conditions both good, we decided to leave the sand hills to the tourists and the touts and head north again to see if it had stopped raining in the mountains. Both Jo and I had done our time sleeping under the stars in the freezing desert and drinking lukewarm Bedouin tea during previous visits to Morocco, and while living in Syria for a couple of years. We didn't need a go-round. Bike riders will understand why we preferred to head back to the mountains, others will just have to figure it out. What should be clear, however, is that we had only the most basic plan for our journey and that we were starting to change the way we related to the places we visited and the journey itself.

We raced back along our route through the Drãa River Valley to the place where we had entered from the west. From here we continued north over the Anti-Atlas mountains to the city of Ouarzazate, then north east up the Dadés River Valley, also known as the Valley of a Thousand Kasbahs. By late afternoon we were looking forward to finding some accommodation for the night when we entered a hilltop village to find the road blocked with a crush of people and the Elephant locked into a press of traffic. Fifteen minutes of manoeuvring got us to the front of the crush where we discovered a big demonstration blocking the central square. We asked a local when the road would be open. 'Maybe tomorrow morning', was the reply.

We pushed and shoved our way back through the traffic then backtracked along the valley for 40 minutes before we found an ageing, icy cold hotel on a hill above El-Kelaa M'Gouna. Although it had been a long day and we were tired, we were still delighted to come across a Berber wedding procession blocking one side of the road. About 50 women with musical instruments paraded the bride along the street on the way to the ceremony. The women's costumes were an explosion of colour and there was much laughing and good humoured capering about to the constant beat of a dozen or more small drums.

It was a great spectacle to see the women out in public enjoying their part of the festivities. Here in the south of Morocco, where the population is nearly all Berber, we found women to be much more prominent in everyday public life. They often spontaneously waved and smiled as we rode through the villages and they were engaged in commerce in one area or another. We didn't see this kind of thing in the Arab dominated north.

In El-Kelaa M'Gouna, we shared our overnight stop with a group of about 16 bike riders from the UK who were spending a week riding dirt bikes in Morocco and following the Paris-Dakar Rally which was scheduled to pass through Morocco not far to the east. They had only been in the country for one day and one rider already had an arm in a sling with little likelihood that he would remount his bike. They were all heartily disillusioned because they had just heard the announcement that the rally had been cancelled for 2007 after three French tourists were shot by terrorists in Senegal.

The Elephant wasn't interested in their skinny-bummed KTMs, so in the morning we left them to it and continued to the east and into the mountain gorges. This part of the country is stunning and the road was constantly framed by the snow covered Atlas and Anti-Atlas mountains, often against the backdrop of the powder-blue Moroccan sky. We loved this area so much we spent a week riding the passes up into the snow-covered mountains through fertile valleys with spectacular old *kasbah*s crumbling on the hill tops. From a base in the town of Tinerhir, we set out to explore in all directions and each day we sought out the mountain roads that clambered up in impossible switchbacks, sometimes treacherous with ice but always breathtaking.

Throughout this period we started to become aware that our journey was changing and we were changing with it. It wasn't something that we discussed much, but Jo's back was improving all the time; I was feeling comfortable riding the bike; and we had started to settle into a rhythm of travelling and 'hunting and gathering' that suited us. The changes had just crept up on us while we were busy with other things and finally surprised us one day in the village of Tinerhir.

The proprietor of the Oasis Hotel had kindly let us park the Elephant in the storeroom and had come around to open the door when we returned from exploring the mountains. With our limited French and his limited English we struck up a conversation.

'Why are you in Morocco?' he asked.

'Oh, we're just looking around,' came the reply.

'Touristic?'

'Oui, touristic.'

'So, where have you been?'

We opened our maps and pointed to the pink highlighted line and date annotations that showed our travels. He studied it closely and asked questions about places and towns.

'Amazing,' he said. 'You have seen more of Maroc than me! Where will you go next?'

We looked at each other, realising we had not yet discussed our next destination.

'Perhaps we will go to the south. Another rider we met in Agadir is down there and he says it is very cheap and there are no tourists,' I said, and looked back over at Jo, who shrugged. 'Or,' I continued, 'we might go north to the Riff and look at the Atlantic Coast.'

He considered this lack of certainty for a few moments then gave a broad smile. 'I think I understand,' he said. 'You are not tourists, you are *voyageurs*!'

His words hit us like a bolt of lightning and made us grin from ear to ear. 'Yes!' we blurted out in unison. 'We are *voyageurs*!'

That night we ate our mutton *tajine* in fine spirits. We had always known intuitively that the idea of a journey was important to us, but now we were starting to understand the reason why it was important. Like most parents we had told our children that life was not a destination but a journey and it was the way that you made that journey that was the measure of who you were. It wasn't that our journey had become an analogue for our life, we simply realised that, in a very practical physical sense, how we travelled was much more important than our destination. We understood in Tinerhir that this doesn't happen often in life and that this was what made it a special time.

In the end, the decision about where we would go next was made by the Elephant. We were still running the same rear tyre we had put on before leaving London and by then we had 15,000 kilometres on it. I carefully measured the remaining tread and worked out that there were about 1500 safe kilometres left; not enough to go south again and get back to Tangier for a replacement. One of our friends pointed out to us in an exchange of emails that 'you won't need tread on dry bitumen', but the experience of having spent weeks riding on wet or icy roads was enough to convince us that there was a hole in this logic. We left the gorges and headed north.

By the afternoon of 9 January we were in Ouarzazate. The Elephant was parked on the veranda of another hotel and we were drinking red wine and talking about riding over the mountains into Marrakech and the other imperial cities of Fès and Meknès. This time we decided we would check the weather report before we started!

Ouarzazate is the home of the Moroccan film industry. It was a spacious modern city with wide avenues and clean, uncluttered public squares. The town has a large film studio and a Moroccan version of a film theme park with fancy horse and camel riding and scenes from the many major films made in the area. The town itself is interesting without being spectacular. It was a comfortable place and we were happy to spend a couple of days there.

To get to Marrakech we needed to cross the High Atlas Mountains through the Tizi n'Tichka Pass at 2264 metres. What looked set to be another tough-ride day turned out to be an easy run. The most recent snow falls were several days past and the ice sheets that form overnight on the corners had been broken up by heavy traffic by the time we arrived. We made good time up to the pass, whipping by the slower traffic, then joined a procession of crawling trucks over the narrow high pass where overtaking on the icy roads was risky. There was, however, plenty of time to look at the glorious scenery as we crawled along.

High in the mountains we stopped at a roadside café when we saw a yellow KTM off-road bike parked outside and a rider seated at a table on the muddy sidewalk. The delicious smell of barbecueing lamb chops was a distraction as we introduced ourselves to Daniele Bonassi, a Swiss rider who had been in Morocco for a couple of weeks and was returning to Marrakech to fly home the next day. The tiny restaurant was a typical roadside stop in these parts of Morocco. The ramshackle wooden structure was fully open to the road down one side with several charcoal grills at one end. In the back corner, a walled off area screened the conveniences and washbasins for the mandatory washing of hands. There were several lamb carcasses hung near the barbecues and a small service area nearby for the preparation of salads. We ordered a *nus-kilo* of lamb, some mint tea and bread and the cook lopped pieces off one of the carcasses and dropped them on the scales until half a kilo had been accounted for. There was never any attempt in these small restaurants to sort the carcass into different cuts for different purposes; it was all just lamb, and it was all just barbecued, but there are few things more delicious than the smell of barbecueing lamb and by the time our plate of assorted bits arrived we were famished. We grabbed up the lamb in our fingers and started to gnaw into the joints, the juice and fat running down our arms.

While we ate we chatted to Daniele and heard about his adventure over many of the roads we had ridden ourselves. As was often the case when we met fellow adventure riders, a bond formed quickly. In some ways these conversations were very soothing for us. Riders never ask each other the standard round of questions that non-riders need to give them a context for the relationship. Much of the experience is already understood and the motivation taken for granted. We had no accommodation organised for Marrakech and neither did Daniele so we exchanged global roaming numbers before he roared off down the mountain and we demolished the rest of our lamb. Looking up from our plates, we saw a group of eight Honda Transalps cruising past, all gleaming clean and carrying no luggage; their leader setting a conservative pace up front. We finished our tea, paid a few dollars for our lunch and set off after them. It seemed like no time at all before we were slipping by the shiny Transalps. We waved to each one as Elephant rumbled by; a behemoth among the spindly Hondas. We imagined most of the riders would have rather tucked in behind Elephant's broad arse and come along for a proper ride in the mountains. That, after all, is what riding in Morocco is about. That, and barbeceued lamb chops by the side of the road!

Ninety minutes later we were in Marrakech. We found the first hotel on our list and it didn't have a room, so we rang Daniele to see if he had had luck. He was only one street away and arrived a few minutes later. He looked at his watch and said 'Hell, you must have been moving', which we took as compliment. We divided the hotels on our list between us, headed off in different directions. Within an hour we had found a good, cheap hotel, phoned Daniele, checked in, changed into walking clothes, met Daniele in the foyer, and set off to explore the city. Some days are diamonds.

The first thing we noticed about Marrakech was the number of tourists, thousands of them everywhere, and the number of touts. We decided to give ourselves a day to explore the city before we pushed on north towards Fès. Our quick dismissal of Morocco's main tourist city may seem a little harsh and we wouldn't want to dissuade anyone else from going. The Marrakech Kasbah is a beehive of colour and commerce with a maze of covered bazaars and narrow lanes large enough to have genuine fun getting lost. The *souk*s overlap, one into the next, with goods of every type spilling across the walkways and traders hawking their wares in ten different languages.

It was a wonderful place with some fantastic things to see and do. The shopping, in particular, was simply the best and several of our friends would have died happy after a day in some of the antique shops. However, being *voyageurs* rather than tourists, we reserved the right to get lost in the *medina* without the aid of a guide if we wanted to. We didn't buy anything, ever, because we had nowhere to carry it, and we really didn't want to mix with tourists because this meant, inevitably, mixing with tourist touts and paying tourist prices. Perhaps this was a selfish or snobbish attitude, but we understood the transaction that took place in these situations and we just didn't feel we needed to be part of it. Our close friends and offspring are never remotely surprised by this. We have, so they say, always been this way.

The 300-kilometre ride north from Marrakech to Beni-Mellal, on a winding road with breathtaking views, was another of those days that left us grasping for superlatives. Beni-Mellal was an average, prosperous, try-hard Moroccan town. A policeman pulled us over on the way in, after I failed to stop at a red signal (it was so dirty and obscured that only the locals knew where it was), and was surprised to learn that we were staying in town. He gave us directions to a hotel and sent us on our way with a smile and a welcome.

There are no touts, tourists or other undesirables in Beni-Mellal. After the being hassled in Marra, no one in Beni-Mellal gave us a second glance. No one offered to guide us (no one cared if we got lost), no one tried to drag us into their shop, offered us tea, wanted to chat to improve their English, or really gave a damn whether we were there or not. We walked the town and had a filling meal of soup and salad and grilled chicken in a crush of local families crammed into a tiny café that was also doing a roaring take-away trade. We relaxed and noted in our journals that all was right with the world, then we were back on the road for the 350-kilometre ride north to Fès.

The road to Fès ran over the Middle Atlas Mountains for most of the distance and through the towns of Azrou and Ifrane, which are the major ski resorts. The latter was built by the French in the 1930s to resemble a European alpine village, which it does in that 'cutsie alpine' way. We stopped there only long enough to get a photograph of Elephant in the snow as this was a long, spectacular, and cold ride. By then, however, we were so used to riding above the snow line that we hustled the Elephant along at a good pace all the way and were into Fès and settled by late afternoon.

The oldest city in Morocco, Fès had fewer tourists than Marra so the touts had to work twice as hard. The place is famous for its leather and the tanneries occupy a large section of the old city.

Tannery work is a filthy business and has left the river and much of the city polluted but there was much to recommend Fès as a better alternative for tourists than Marrakech. The old *medina* was just as exotic with fewer people to share it with; prices carried less of a tourist-loading; and accommodation was cheap and easy to find. The touts, however, were the most determined we had come across outside of Cairo.

Sixty kilometres west of Fès, the old Imperial City of Meknès was a sleepy backwater with few tourists but some great history. It had a busy but easy to navigate *medina*. We liked the easy pace of Meknès so decided to lay-up there for a few days to do some planning for the next leg of our travels. Meknès was a centre for traditional cedar carving and a type of work with silver inlaid on iron. We met one gentleman who had made an order of 22 silver-inlaid iron kangaroos for a customer in Sydney. Meknès didn't have much of a tourist face, but there was plenty of Moroccan real-life down in the metal workers' *souk* where about 30 small jobbing shops made all manner of household goods from steel.

Our great culinary adventure in Meknès was the discovery of a type of pastry exclusive to this area. It looks like an overgrown éclair complete with sticky icing but is made with a more substantial pastry and filled with a vast quantity of almond or chocolate filling. They were so large that we barely managed to share one between us, and so sweet that we had to wash it down with several cups of strong black coffee. We tended to eat as much interesting and different stuff as we could find on the road, but we put the Meknès pastry into the category of 'it's OK, but we wouldn't bother with it again'. A lot of stuff eventually went into this category.

Our lay up in Meknès allowed us to make a day-trip to the

Roman ruins of Volubilis just north of town. The Romans came here to grow wheat, and when we saw Volubilis sitting above a fertile plain of broad-acre wheat production, we could see the point of the venture. Volubilis was noted for its well-preserved murals. In one, a man sat backwards on a horse holding a cup, which we assumed he had won for trick riding! We enjoyed Volubilis very much. With no timetable and few other visitors, we were able to wander the ruins with our guidebook and gradually identify the nitty gritty of life in a Roman North African city; a subject that was to be an important interest during our further African travels.

Our time in Meknès also allowed us to finally settle our way forward from Morocco. We had intended to ship the Elephant along the coast past Algeria to Tunisia and fly over to Tunis ourselves. This plan, however, proved to be unworkable. The days of coastal freight along the North African coast were long gone. In four weeks of looking we failed to find a single option that didn't containerise the bike and ship it via a European hub, and air freight was equally unlikely. There were no direct flights between the two countries and all air services shipped via a European hub (generally Turin) and the cost for both freight and tax was ridiculous: one arm and one leg... each! The only economically viable option was to cross back to Europe then catch a ferry out of Marseille to Tunisia. The first step was to get back to Europe. We knew there was a ferry out of Nador on the Moroccan Atlantic coast to Sète in France so that would be our first option. If this proved unworkable, then it would be back to southern Spain to transit the 1500 kilometres to Marseille on the motorways before catching a ferry to Tunisia. The final leg of our Moroccan journey, therefore, would take us up and over the Riff Mountains and along the Mediterranean coast to Nador. If we were unable to get a ferry from there, then we would ride back to Tangier. It was late January and the middle of winter so whichever way we went we were going to get cold. Resigned to the inevitable, we rode north across the plains towards the legendary Riff Mountains.

The Riff Mountains were different to every other part of Morocco we had visited. The place had a 'Wild West' feel to it and we got the impression that central government control was limited. We arrived in Nador on 21 January after an exhilarating ride through the mountains and started searching out ferry passage to Sète immediately and found that we were not able to get passage to France for another week. A quick look around convinced us that Nador wasn't the sort of town we wanted to idle away our time in, so we decided on an alternative plan and headed north along the rugged Mediterranean coast to overnight at the town of Al Hoceima before pressing on to Tangier.

We were parked in the main street, studying the map and deciding which of the unattractive accommodation options we would take, when a fellow asked if we needed help. Within a few minutes we knew that Stephane was French and that he was working in Al Hoceima for two years attached to the Moroccan Navy from the French Marines. After considering the accommodation options, Stephane offered us his spare room and organised a garage for Elephant.

Once we had stowed our gear, Stephane gave us a guided tour of the town and the waterfront. Al Hoceima was clustered along the high cliffs overlooking the Mediterranean and around a tiny bay and harbour. The place looked prosperous and there were a number of new developments underway. We ended our wandering at the port where we selected some fish from the fishermen on the docks. These were then handed over to a nearby restaurant for preparation. Of course we had selected more fish than we could possibly eat and when it was presented together with a range of salads, we could hardly make a dent in it. Still, with plenty of cold local beer to wash it down, we did our best. The walk home up a steep track from the waterfront was a challenge with full bellies and fuzzy heads.

Stephane and I had some background in common so we had plenty to talk about (apart from Morocco) and he was also astute enough to lay-in a couple of cold beers back at the apartment to lubricate the conversation. Jo retired to bed and left us to it. Stephane was a wonderful host and, as this was to be our last night in Morocco, we couldn't have had better company or a better time to remember.

The next morning with thick tongues and fuzzy heads, we said farewell to Stephane and headed into the Riff Mountains for the gruelling 8-hour ride to Tangier, hoping the cold morning air would clear our heads. It was a long day and we made very few stops along the way as the area is heavily populated and everywhere we stopped we were approached by young men hoping to sell us some dope, which was the main cash crop of the area. We pushed on to arrive in Tangier just before last light.

Tangier looked no more inviting in the late afternoon than it had in the morning six weeks earlier when we arrived. We made straight for the docks and purchased a ticket on a fast ferry to Spain. Jo fought it out in the passport line while I manoeuvred the Elephant through the traffic jam and we were on the ferry a few minutes later. After six weeks our Moroccan adventure was over.

By 9pm on 24 January we had cleared Spanish immigration

and were heading for a hotel. It would be another three hours of hard riding before we were settled in an expensive European hotel consoling ourselves that at least the plumbing worked.

Morocco had lived up to its reputation as a paradise for bike riders. The amazing mountain and desert roads were a delight and Moroccan food well deserved its reputation as tasty and healthy. The people were genuinely friendly and hospitable; there was none of the anti-western rub we had experienced elsewhere; there was little crime and no alcohol induced violence; and we had felt very much at home there. We stayed longer than we had planned to, and had been reluctant to leave. We made ourselves a promise that that would not be our last winter in Morocco. There was simply too much more to do there.

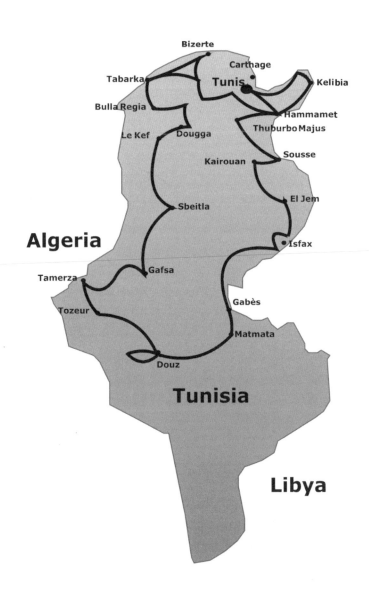

Bizerte

Carthage

Tabarka

Tunis

Kelibia

Bulla Regia

Hammamet

Le Kef

Dougga

Thuburbo Majus

Kairouan

Sousse

Sbeitla

El Jem

Algeria

Isfax

Tamerza

Gafsa

Gabès

Tozeur

Matmata

Douz

Tunisia

Libya

7

Tunisia

Back in Europe, with Euro prices weighing down the budget and the winter weather set in, we had plenty of incentive to get on with our transit leg with urgency. The Elephant is not the best machine for highway running but the 1650-kilometre run was gobbled up comfortably in three chilly days, putting us in Marseille on the afternoon of 27 January 08. This gave us a couple of days before the next ferry in which to relax and get and some important jobs done.

Marseille seemed like a useful, rough and ready sort of city. It had some welcoming public spaces and some very elegant streets, as well as some very run down areas and more than its share of beggars. We felt pretty comfortable there. We particularly liked the wide avenues of nineteenth century apartments that linked the city with the port. A concerted effort was underway to restore the façades of these and, as many of them were gutted in the process, we assumed there was internal renewal as well. The gentrification still had a way to run, but there was no doubt that the result would be a particularly beautiful and functional city.

By now the Elephant's tyres were pretty much gone. What little rubber that was left after Morocco had quickly disappeared on the freeways up through Spain. On the rainy streets of Marseille, the back-end was feeling decidedly skittish but, as we joked while we hurried through the drizzle, you don't need tread on dry bitumen. Our first stop was the bike souq for a new set of Michelin Anakees, and there we said goodbye to US$550!

Tyres are very important to bikes. On a big bike they are under great stress and wear out much quicker than car tyres. Experienced riders can feel the difference between tyres through the seat of their pants in seconds and never stop talking about this. The last set of Anakees lasted 19,000 kilometres on the back and 28,000 kilometres on the front; the best wear I have ever had from a tyre for a big bike. We did some mileage calculations and hoped the new tyres would get us home. We couldn't have know then that Russia would make nonsense of these calculations. In fact, Russia would make nonsense of many things.

We also took the opportunity to look at some new riding suits. We were unhappy with ours, and talked to every other rider we met about their choice of suit. These investigations eventually lead us to the Hein Gerick outlet to see the suits that were most often recommended, which didn't disappoint but at US$1750 each were way outside our budget. We decided to put up with the suits we had. In hindsight we had skimped on this important equipment before the trip and shouldn't have done so. After all, we were wearing our riding suits all day, every day we were on the road.

We used the remainder of our time in Marseille to organise our Tunis ferry tickets, do some banking, catch up on correspondence and get used to dodging dog shit on the French footpaths again. We also caught up on a little sleep as we had declined to pay the extra US$200 for a cabin for the overnight ferry to Tunis. We expected the trip over to be tiring, but we didn't plan on what happened next.

Our loading instructions were to be at the wharf by 10am for immigration and check-in before loading at noon and sailing at 2pm. As it turned out, we cleared immigration by 10.10am and then sat for four and a half hours waiting to load.

There were long lines of vehicles, many of them old sedans, overloaded with all manner of household and consumer goods being taken back by returning Tunisians. Many of the loads had shifted on the trip to the docks with some hanging precariously over the side of the vehicles and causing them to list badly. We had a little entertainment watching the slapstick that was the repacking. The day was bitterly cold and we were thoroughly chilled by the time we rolled on board.

Seating conditions on board were similar to those on an aircraft but, as the ship was less than half full, there was enough room to sleep on the floor between the rows of seats and we both got more sleep than we usually do on a long haul flight, but that was not much. We were both looking forward to a shower and a change of clothes by the time we docked in Tunis.

I was travelling on an EU passport so had no visa requirements for Tunisia but Jo was not so lucky with her passport. She had discovered that Australian citizens could buy a 90-day visa at the point of entry for about US$6 (Canadians and New Zealanders likewise, but all other non-EU citizens required a visa in advance). However, when she presented her passport to the police onboard the ship, she found that it was not going to be that easy. The police kept her passport and told her to report to the police post at the port to see about the visa. Finding the police was no problem (they were everywhere) and she even located her passport again, but getting the visa was more difficult. We spent the next two and a half hours with the Elephant parked in the middle of the road and the two of us stood waiting while the problem was sorted. We had found that the best way forward in these situations was mostly to stay very calm and to be very patient. This was not the same as being passive. Good-humoured persistence was also important. From our observations, the quickest way to be put to the back of the queue was to get angry and raise your voice. Petty bureaucrats are the same the world over. They can't abide a challenge to their authority but are very keen to get rid of a nuisance.

Eventually the passport arrived with a visa, at a price of US$35 for 30 days, and we were free to enter Tunisia. We rumbled up the causeway from the port with Elephant wallowing along in the teeming sea of humanity that is the city of Tunis. We enjoyed the moment, if for no other reason than that it had taken us six expensive days to get there.

After our initial introduction to Tunisian bureaucracy, the country lived up, and down, to our expectations. Jo and the Elephant (being aliens) could only get 30 days on their visas, and with the ferry schedule reduced in winter, we needed to keep moving to get a handle on the country and get out on time. As soon as we had found a cheap hotel and washed off the travel grime we spread out our maps and started on our Tunisian plan.

Tunisia has about 3000 years of recorded history, much of it Punic and Roman. I have always had an interest in these periods since studying Ancient History in school 40 years previously. The Punic wars, in particular, had also been a source of great misery, as I had studied Latin, too, and they were the subject of endless translations from Latin to English. We decided that this would be a good theme for our visit to Tunisia and planned our route around the major sites.

As always, our plan was simple. We would spend a few days

in Tunis to see the city, the Bardo Museum, and the ruins at Carthage, and from there we would do a clockwise circuit of the country ending back at Tunis in about three weeks.

Much of the history of Tunisia is contained in a large number of archaeological sites across the country. As these were excavated, many of the important finds were removed for display to the Bardo Museum in the capital. The Bardo and the ruins of ancient Carthage, which are now in the northern suburbs, were excuse enough to stay over a few days in Tunis.

From our comfortable, friendly pub close to the centre of town, we started to get a feel for Tunis. It was a grand old city but also a city out of all proportion with the country it serves. As with a lot of small countries, Tunis is the only major city of Tunisia. It dwarfs every other town and is unlike every other town. The old city was well preserved and ultimately a little touristy. The new city had wide tree lined avenues, flash hotels and smart restaurants. It was a bustling, noisy, smelly and chaotic place, which we like in a big city, and we wandered around mostly ignored by the throng. The locals hustled for a dollar and the usual tourist touts did their best to make sure visitors contributed generously to the tourism industry. As always, we must have been a disappointment as we slouched around the back streets with the locals.

Among the hustle and hum of a city we found plenty of cafés and restaurants for every taste and price level. Generally, we settled for the cheap-eats; the back-street restaurants, where we began to explore the local food and asked the locals where we should go and what we should see in their country. It was a comfortable, easy-going start.

As soon as we had sorted the basics of life in Tunisia, we headed for the Bardo Museum. It is some distance out of the city and we found our way there on the tram system, which was cheap and efficient and took us meandering around the suburbs. As always, there was simple delight in rubbing along with folk going about their daily business, particularly as we didn't have any of our own.

The museum was well maintained and had a stunning collection that was well presented. The highlight of the museum was undoubtedly the many Roman mosaics rescued from archaeological sites. These North African works have a unique style and are, in our uneducated view, superior to those we had seen in Europe. We liked one depicting a scene from the Odyssey in particular as Jo and I had been members of the Ulysses motorbike Club for some time. To be a full member of the club you needed to be 50 years of age. The club's name reflects the ageing Ulysses who, having returned to the faithful Penelope and settled his kingdom, was restless and longed to go adventuring with his ship-mates one more time. The mosaic told the story of Ulysses and the sirens. In the legend, any sailor who heard the sirens' song, or laid eyes on them, would be drawn to his death. To avoid this, Ulysses had himself tied to the ship's mast while the Argonauts had their ears stuffed with wax and were ordered to look away. The cunning Ulysses was terribly tormented, but he and the lads survived. I'm not sure what the moral of the story is, but, as any Ulyssesian will attest, experience and rat-cunning always overcomes youth and enthusiasm in the end.

For the ruins of Carthage, we again caught a tram and then a suburban train. Once again the system was cheap and worked fine, even if it was crowded. Although it was Sunday and officially a holiday, a few classes of school kids descended on Carthage while we were there. Jo, who has had plenty of experience in these matters, reckons they were about as interested in the exhibits as most school kids on most excursions. I took this to mean that they would rather have been elsewhere.

The ruins were spread over a wide area and we decided to walk between them to get some codgercise. This made it easy for us to drop into the American War Cemetery located in the same area as the ruins. Like the many Commonwealth cemeteries we have visited, it was beautifully maintained and tranquil. In the summer, bus loads of American tourists descend on the place from the cruise ships that ply the Med but the day we were there the place was eerily quiet.

Our first days in Tunisia were easy enough, but we were disappointed to find that the Tunisians were as hopeless as plumbers as the Moroccans and the Spanish (and to some extent the French, who probably taught them everything they knew). Basically, nothing worked properly. Drains didn't drain and everything that gets the water to the drain was ad hoc and poorly maintained.

Knowing how well the Romans had managed the hydraulics of their towns, we decided to focus our historic investigation a little and to try to discover some Tunisian plumbing history on our travels. This was to become a running joke as we travelled on in North Africa, and then through Russia and beyond. We decided that the start of the Dark Ages was not presaged by the fall of the Roman Empire, but by the disbanding of the Plumbers' Guild.

Looking for hydraulic answers, we loaded Elephant and headed north-east out of Tunis towards Cap Bon and the Phoenician site of Kerkouane. On the way we started getting used to Tunisian road conditions and it wasn't long before we had found the horrible truth about Tunisian road behaviour. In Tunisia, the only things with any road sense were the camels, which hated Elephants and always gave us a wide berth. To be fair, the sheep were also pretty good at staying off the road. The humans, on the other had, were suicidal! We were yet to meet many locals but already we were keen to know why they stepped onto the road without checking for traffic and walked diagonally across with their backs to the traffic. It seemed like foolish bravado at first impression, but we felt sure there were other factors in the mix.

Despite our misgivings about our fellow road users and the caution it instilled in Team Elephant, we were not long in finding the first entry for our Tunisian Plumbing Tour guidebook. 2500 years ago, in an idyllic spot by the sea, the Phoenicians built a small trading town at Kerkouane. The town is so ancient that its original name has been lost but the ruins were amazingly preserved and easy to access.

It didn't take us long to find the evidence of antecedent Tunisian hydraulic engineers. The town had reticulated water from a spring through an aqueduct to a cistern and on to bathrooms. Water was moved through standard sections of channel, which were mass-produced. Laundries and commercial washing facilities were joined to the system, while the poor had access to communal latrines and wash houses. Storm water ran off through guttering and collectors to end up in a sewerage outlet to the sea some distance away. It was elegant!

Further south at the much more recent Roman site of Thuburbo Maius we were free to wander the archaeological site without restriction. Here we found huge cisterns fed by an aqueduct from mountain springs 40 kilometres away, and wide streets with drains running under them. There were all manner of plumbing fixtures, with heated baths for the winter and non-heated ones for the summer. Large areas of the 'wet floors' were covered with mosaics and the storm water drains were sophisticated enough to filter the rubbish.

The same aqueduct that serviced Thuburbo Maius ran more than 130 kilometres across the country and fed the mighty cisterns of Carthage, which were nearly a kilometre in length and very impressive. At El Jem we visited the huge colosseum and the site of some Roman houses nearby, where we found an elaborate system for collecting and filtering rainwater using standard plumbing fittings, including joining- and T-pieces, made of lead. The water was collected in a series of ponds that overflowed one into another to settle and clear, with the excess water flowing onto the gardens. To top it off, the pond surrounds were used as garden spaces and were decorated with beautiful mosaics. All of these ancient waterworks provided an elegant solution to the city's shortage of water so don't ask me why, 2000 years later, we were hard pressed to find a pub with drains that drained.

Having gotten our gripe about the plumbing off our chests, we started to focus on the things about Tunisia that matter, like whether we could get a cold beer at the end of a long ride. The answer to that, like with many things in Tunisia, was 'yes…and no'.

Tunisia is a small country. It is about the size of Victoria, Australia; Washington State, USA; or England and Wales combined. Too many long days in the saddle here, and you would run out of space. There are a few mountains, with the high bits in the north, and the south is given over to flat plains running off into the Sahara. The big cities and the population are gathered along the northern and eastern coastlines, along with the major tourist developments.

After our loop around Cap Bon to the north east of Tunis, we ran down the heavily populated eastern coast in no time at all, before crossing inland through the dusty towns on the edge of the Sahara. That's half way around the country. The coastal towns were geared up for tourists and in some towns there were a lot of Germans managing to dress for summer while we were wearing puffer jackets.

The usual tourist cycle was a holiday by the sea punctuated by organised bus excursions to the interior sites. The country was small enough to avoid many overnight stays in the smaller internal towns. El Jem, for instance, one of the largest colosseums built by the Romans, was right in the middle of the town and an amazing site, but there was not much accommodation nearby. Most visitors come in from the coast on a day trip. Some of the inland hotels had been built in the French era, before the coastal tourism boom and had fallen on hard times in the bus-in tourism age. They were, however, inevitably helpful in securing the Elephant, often by allowing us to park it in the foyer. That is, if I could ride it up a flight of stairs!

As we rode south we found that Tunisia had some very fertile areas, but that much of the country was marginal for agriculture. Considerable ingenuity had been used in the traditional farming practices of the area. In some areas, compensation dams were used to trap the run-off top-soil and grow crops in the inhospitable central hills. In other areas, contour walls trapped rainfall on the wet side of the mountains and moved it to the side that didn't get rain.

Interestingly, Tunisia, used by the Romans as the bread basket for the empire, imported 40 percent of its food and didn't grow enough wheat for its own needs. The price of bread, however, was government subsidised and formed an important part of every meal. Unfortunately, the bread was universally made from processed white flour so this was not a win for good nutrition.

Away from the coast, much of the landscape was pretty tough and temperatures were extreme. It wasn't surprising that in some areas of the interior, troglodyte houses were built under ground to avoid the summer heat. When we visited these areas, however, it was so cold that we were looking for a place in the sun.

Further out, the hills washed out into the edge of the Sahara and dissipated into broad salt lakes. Near the town of Tozeur, we followed one track across the salt for kilometres. We eventually came to a small sand rise and a tiny oasis. Four young men were working on a basic accommodation building around which they hoped to build a tourism venture. Beyond their tiny oasis the track petered out and the sand hills of the Sahara rolled away to the ends of the earth. We stopped for a chat and Jo dismounted so that I could gun the Elephant around on the soft sand. We wished them well with their venture and they wished us well with ours before we turned north across the salt plains and back towards civilization.

Along the edge of the desert we found small towns gathered around each oasis eking out a living on the edge of emptiness. The small desert fringe towns were generally a collection of low, mud brick houses and one or two more modern steel or concrete structures. Often a school was the most substantial building in the village. The brown dust was everywhere and the blowing sands of the Sahara constantly threatened to overwhelm the narrow roads and low houses.

Life has always been precarious here but one day we found a lunar-scape of ruins that demonstrated how precarious. In 1979 unusually heavy rains had simply washed away the mud houses of the town and it was never occupied again.

After Tozeur, we explored to the west until we reached the Algerian border and could go no further. Near the border there was a big police and military presence and lots of roadblocks so we didn't take photos in this area. In general, we were waved through the checkpoints but occasionally we were stopped and questioned before being waved on our way, always with a smile and a 'welcome to Tunisia'.

By the second week of February we had nowhere else to go in the south west and turned north into the rolling hills of the centre seeking out the important archaeological sites of Dougga and Bulla Regia and an interesting route back to the north coast. Our journey was going well but we had been in Tunisia for three weeks and still hadn't fully sorted out the critical issue of getting a cold beer at the end of a long ride.

We had found out by then that the Tunisians make a quite acceptable local beer and at least one very drinkable red wine. The only problem was getting to them! Licensing was expensive and only the up-market restaurants served alcohol. We usually didn't eat at such places. When we did find one that was convenient and decided to treat ourselves, a couple of Celtia beers and a bottle of Magon vin rouge was just the trick. Although, in most cases, the beer was cool but not cold.

Apart from the top restaurants, there were café bars in most towns. Unfortunately, these were full of blokes and cigarette smoke. The only ladies we saw in them were 'working'. The better option for us was to buy a bottle of wine and have a couple of drinks in our room before dinner then a nightcap when we returned. The only trouble with this option was finding a bottle shop! Most towns had one, but it was generally a nondescript shop in a back street and we usually came across them by chance. In the big cities, some of the supermarkets also had a small alcohol selection but we didn't have the capacity on the Elephant to carry supplies.

As we headed north from Tozeur on the edge of the Sahara, one of our objectives was to end three days of abstention in the southern towns (a trip record up to then) so we arrived late into the town of Sbeitla with expectations. We selected the cheaper of the two available hotels, the only one within budget, and found the closest thing to a restaurant for a chicken and *frittes* dinner. Back at our hotel, we found the bar full of smoke and pissed workmen, so I took a couple of cheap beers back to our (thankfully) warm room. It was hardly a grand celebration, but it was a start.

The catering arrangements notwithstanding, Sbeitla was high on our must-see list. It was the site of extensive Roman ruins with some of the best features of Roman towns including a grid pattern of wide streets, baths with under-floor heating and beautiful mosaic floors still being walked on after 2,000 years. Like most of these sites, Sbeitla had a number of owners after its architects had been moved on. The Vandals came and, well, vandalised the place. Then the Byzantines demonstrated their comparative lack of skill as engineers and builders by rearranging the Roman stone work in most unfortunate ways. Later came the Ottomans and the Arabs, but the city had lost its lustre by then.

Moving north from Sbeitla, we were chased into the town of Le Kef by some ferociously cold and wet weather. We used the weather as an excuse for a lay-up day and found a hotel in the middle of town with heating (of sorts) and a warm sunny room. They were good enough to put out a ramp for me to get the bike into the foyer. You don't get that kind of service at home!

By this stage on our journey, I had become quite adept at riding the bike fully laden up steps to park it inside buildings. Nonetheless, these exercises were always challenging. I managed to keep Elephant on its wheels for the most part, but the few occasions we fell occurred trying to get up steps and inside a pub, or rolling off the centre stand in a service station.

The weather cleared and we were able to see the local sites and do some 'make and mend'. Le Kef had some old Roman ruins right in amongst the modern town, an interesting fort overlooking the city that was built by the Byzantines and has been upgraded by each new owner up to the current Tunisian Army.

The town also had a very good folk museum with a range of Berber cultural displays. The day we went was freezing cold and the manager was happy to keep warm by taking us on an extended tour of the exhibits. My favourite item was a woven cover to keep the camels' humps warm in winter. Apparently they got grumpy when cold; like elephants I suppose.

Through all of this, we had been rubbing along pretty well with our Tunisian hosts. Big bikes like ours were very uncommon in Tunisia, so we certainly got noticed wherever we went. I am surprised that Jo's arm didn't fall off as she spent so much time waving to folks of all ages as we passed through the countryside. When we stopped, young fellows would come over to look at the numbers on the speedo. I didn't have the heart to tell them how optimistic they were with our big luggage fit. The guys always asked how big the motor was and the answer of 1150cc left them with a stunned look on their faces.

With our riding suits, helmets, incomprehensible language, GPS and communications setup, we might as well have been space travellers in some remote villages. Here, even more so than in Morocco, we were a curiosity. We were, however, clearly strangers and clearly on a grand journey, something easily understood by these desert peoples with their long tradition of respect for travellers. Tunisians, we had discovered, were also some of the most demonstrative people we had come across. Any two Tunisian friends having a chat over coffee were like six of our taciturn countrymen lining up for a fist-fight! Until we got used to it, it seemed like everyone was arguing with everyone else all the time. None of this, however, was reflected in the way we, and other visitors, were treated.

In Le Kef, I needed to do some repairs to our helmet wiring looms. These were the cables that linked the speakers and microphones in our helmets with the intercom system on the bike. We had worn out a set each because of the constant flexing of the main cable where it exited the helmet. I went to a little hardware store and explained the problem to the owner with a little engineering drawing and a few words of French. He and his assistant went to work finding parts that I might adapt to my needs and after 30 minutes and several revised drawings assembled the selection of bits.

When I asked him how much, he handed me the parts and with a broad smile, said there was no charge and; 'welcome to Tunisia'. We smiled back our most thankful smiles and shook everyone's hand before taking our paper bag of bits back to the hotel to start work on the helmet repair.

It was through small kindnesses such as these that North Africa became the place where we started to understand something of the transaction we were involved in each time we interacted with local people. We started to say that we were 'pushed on by the kindness of strangers', and this was certainly true, but it was not the whole story. We found that each transaction involved an exchange. We would offer our story; the story of strangers and an odyssey, and in return they would offer kindness and their hopes for the success of our journey. In the final part of the transaction, we would take their wishes and add them to the others we carried with us. Each time we told the story of our journey in return for a favour done, we carried forward the expectations of yet another soul. For it seemed that the idea of the journey transcended culture and that there was a universal belief that to journey among strangers is an honourable thing; a thing worth doing for its own sake.

When we started our journey our goals were poorly defined and a little vague. We wanted to ride to Vladivostok but secretly we had decided that we would go on until it got too difficult or we just didn't want to do it any more. We lacked confidence in our ability and didn't want to raise the expectations of our friends or, in truth, ourselves. There was no point, we rationalised, in doing something just to say you had done it. One night in Le Kef I reminded Jo of a meeting we had had in Morocco. In late January 2008, on a rainy Tuesday, we stopped at a busy, muddy intersection at a small market town in the south of the Riff Mountains. The policeman on duty saw us stop and check the road in both directions obviously considering which way to go. He left his post and walked over to us and signalled the question 'can I help?' We confirmed the direction we needed to take. He then indicated the broader question, 'where are you going?'. We told him our story in a few mixed words of English, French and Arabic, together with a lot of sign language. A huge smile came over his face:

'So, you and your wife go on your bike. You go to all the world's countries and see all the world's peoples. Good luck! Good luck!'

Perhaps that night, I said to Jo, he went home to his little daughter and said something along the lines of: 'you will never guess what happened today. A man and a woman came to our town. They were wearing space suits and riding on a puny elephant with spindly legs and a funny snout. They told me they were going to see all of the world's peoples and all of their places. I gave them a gift. I gave them a smile and a wish, and they said that they would carry it over the Riff, over the high mountains, across the endless wheat plains and through the forest of the bear. And they said that they would take it to the warm Pacific and cast it into the air and it would float back to me.'

After this we had changed. With our saddlebags full of the expectations of others, willingly accepted, we knew then we would go to Vladivostok, or break ourselves or Elephant trying.

North from Le Kef, with our newly-repaired helmets, we set out to visit two important Roman sites in a single day so that we could push on and find some decent accommodation on the north coast. The site at Dougga was nestled into the hills near the modern town of Teboursouk. Like most of these settlements, the Roman inhabitants were replaced by a succession of others who mistreated the original design in one way or another. Apparently local farming folk had been living among the ruins up until the mid-1950s when they were resettled nearby.

The ruins contained extensive noteworthy mosaics. But, as always, I loved the plumbing best. We found an amazing 12-seat public latrine that was a hoot. The Romans obviously didn't have any qualms about literally rubbing shoulders with their neighbours while on the job. We could imagine the sorts of banal conversations that would have taken place with a full house of a dozen bums straining over the stream of water that would carry away their waste; sorting out the day's priorities while taking care of the morning's priority.

We didn't linger at Dougga as we had heard that Bulla Regia was worth a longer visit. We had a quick lunch in the car park then scarpered over the hills and on to Bulla Regia with the weather closing in again. The Bulla Regia site did not look too exciting at first glance and it wasn't until we walked over the ruins that we found its secret.

The villas at Bulla Regia were built with the living quarters below ground-level to avoid the summer heat. These were classic Roman villas, with a central courtyard, but just sunk into the earth. The bathrooms, latrines and kitchens (all the smelly bits) were above ground with the bedrooms and living areas below. This was also the site of the best mosaics we had seen outside the museums. The detail in some of them was bright and fresh and seeing them on the original floors that they were laid on gave us an eerie feeling. Some were a little damaged but others had almost complete detail. Walking over a 2000-year old mosaic of such exquisite beauty seemed shocking at first but, on reflection, the floors had been laid to be walked on and a hundred generations had done just that. These mosaics were more stunning on the ground at Bulla Regia, still being used as floors, than they ever could have been on a wall in the Bardo Museum.

By the time we got away from Bulla Regia the bad weather had caught up and the rain had started. We headed up into the hills and through the cloud base, passed the old French hill-station of Ain Draham, with the rain chasing us down onto the coastal plain and into the north coast town of Tabarka and a warm dry room. We stayed only a night at Tabarka before deciding that it was not our favourite part of Tunisia, then swept back to the east coast, by-passing Tunis, looking for a bolt-hole to rest and plan the next leg of our journey.

146

We spent our last week in Tunisia at the faded seaside town of Hammamet in a comfortable apartment with a sitting room overlooking a courtyard with a large fig tree that was the night roost for hundreds of noisy sparrows. This part of the Tunisian coast had been discovered by wealthy Europeans during the 1930s and the long established tourist areas had been around long enough to run down. In the area we stayed, the hotels would have been in their prime forty years before and were now used for cheap package weeks for Northern Europeans seeking a break from the grind of the winter.

Down the coast another fifteen kilometres newer resorts catered to richer tourists. The streets were lined with expensive restaurants and the marinas were crammed with expensive yachts. It was from these safe havens that the bussed-in tourists descended on the historic sites of the interior only to disappear again without making much of an impact on the local economy.

In our faded hotel we had a lazy week of late coffee and pastry breakfasts and after dinner strolls for gelato. We leavened this with vigorous 2-hour walks each day to make sure we felt virtuous enough to indulge. Jo's back hadn't returned to full strength, but it was improving each day and she was feeling confident that she could avoid a recurrence of the injury. Exercise and rest, both in good measure, seemed to have a healing effect.

Apart from giving us a rest after many weeks of almost constant movement, the break gave us some time for reflection on our Tunisian sojourn. It also marked the first six months of our journey. We had felt comfortable and at home in Tunisia. The Tunisians were good hosts and the country, while lacking the drama of Morocco, had some wonderful sights, particularly in the deserted south. Tunisia certainly provided a better desert experience than the over-exploited patch of sand that passed for the Moroccan desert.

The archaeological sites were stunning and numerous and were the highlight for us both. Visiting in the dead of winter we often had these places to ourselves with plenty of time to look for the small detail that gave a clue to the lives of the original inhabitants. Grand temples, we decided, were all well and good, but the real story of those who built and used them was more often in the plumbing!

We had also continued to eat simply but well in Tunisia. The food was probably less distinctive than Moroccan fare but we could generally go to bed with full bellies for a few dollars. The small local restaurants all had basically the same menu and similar prices and all had at least one television in the corner at full volume. Even the better quality eateries had their blaring television set as a constant distraction. We had not had the opportunity to visit the homes of ordinary Tunisians, but we were left wondering if television dominated their homes in a similar way.

The Tunisians ate tinned tuna with almost everything. It dressed all salads, came on pizzas, and was an essential ingredient in most fast-food and all sandwiches. It even replaced the anchovies in puttanesca sauce. Sacrilege! Jo had always been happy enough to eat tinned fish but I have avoided it as far as possible. It is not that I find it objectionable, it is simply that it reminds me of my time as a young National Serviceman. At that time there were not many options in the combat ration packs but one was a large can of tuna. I once had seven of these packs in row and it cured me of tinned fish for life.

Jo also discovered a peculiarity of Tunisian cuisine obviously intended for no other reason than to catch out the traveller. She ordered *tajine* early in our stay, expecting the usual hearty dish of vegetables and meat that we had enjoyed in Morocco. She was surprised to find that Tunisian *tajines* were like a *frittata* and were made of eggs and leftovers!

We had also seen, and been seen by, a measurable percentage of Tunisia's school children. There were three levels of schooling in Tunisia from the primary kids with kid-size bags to the young adults doing the four-year International Baccalaureate. Each of these groups had two sessions of schooling a day and the start times for the classes were staggered. This meant that all day, from 7am to 6pm, there were kids going to or from school and, since Tunisians only walked on the roadway, riding through any town was a slow process of weaving through throngs of young pedestrians. They did, however, look well fed, smartly turned out and happy, all of which was a delight.

So, we had a good time in Tunisia overall. But we did have one gripe. Tunisians were, in our experience, the world's best litterers. Our previous record holders were the Syrians, who found innumerable new and interesting ways to dress the landscape with plastic bags, but these folk were a cut above that standard. The Tunisian president had launched an anti-litter campaign but it was still to have an impact on the behaviour of the people. It was commonplace to see a parent unwrap a sweet for a child and throw the paper on the ground. People of all ages, both genders and all social classes acted with the same assurance that they had a perfect right to turn the land into a rubbish dump. They didn't seem to see the rubbish or care about it.

The major urban and tourist areas were kept clean by armies of street sweepers who worked throughout the night to get things tidied up for the morning but out of these areas, where there was no clean-up service, the rubbish just mounted up and no one seemed to care. In many small towns the inhabitants literally lived in a stinking rubbish dump of their own making.

This is not to say that the people or their houses were dirty. Far from it, they were invariably clean and well presented. It is just that no one felt any responsibility for those spaces that were not their direct property.

For us as travellers, this was a complete pain in the arse. No one wants to stop for a break in a rubbish heap, but any area that could be used as a stop would invariably be filthy. The Tunisians can't blame this state of affairs on anyone else. We'd encountered plenty of poorer people who managed to keep their environment neat and tidy.

Our Tunisian adventure ended pretty much as it began with a long wait at a ferry terminal and Elephant strapped down in the belly of a ship. Spring was on the way and we needed to go north into Central Europe and on to Russia. Although the ferry passage was only 10 hours from Tunis to Palermo in Sicily, we paid the extra for a cabin. We expected the ferry to be more crowded than the trip over from Marseille, and sleeping upright in a chair hadn't worked for either of us on that voyage. On board the ferry, Eurostar Salerno, we had a beer with Sicilian BMW rider Vito and his wife Antonella, then retired to our cabin and drifted into a peaceful sleep, blissfully unaware that the Italian border police would find new and interesting ways to confuse us in just a few hours' time.

8

Long Days in Short Countries

The ferry-passage from Tunis to Palermo, Sicily, was smooth and we slept well in our comfortable cabin. Next morning, we rose and packed early to be ready for the formalities of getting back into the EU. Our experience on these ferries so far had been that the immigration procedures were carried out on board and in transit to shorten the turn around in port. We selected a strategic place and waited for the action to begin but the desks and chairs set up in the passageway for this purpose remained empty.

The chairs were still empty as the ferry backed into the Palermo dock. The crew were inscrutable and insisted in herding passengers into the ship's cafeteria, but we hung back resisting all efforts to direct us into the masses. We didn't know what the format for the proceedings would be, but experience had taught us not to be timid at these times. When Vito and Antonella appeared at our elbow and confirmed that we were aimed at the right doorway for EU passport holders, we pushed forward with renewed determination. We stood our ground against the others now jostling us and relentlessly shoved aside those with less mass or determination.

We were amongst the first dozen to be processed by a disinterested, harassed looking official, but it had taken nearly an hour in the throng to get through. We could only imagine how long it took for those starting back in the cafeteria mass. We rolled Elephant down the ramp from the vehicle deck and straight into the streets of Palermo. I think I heard Elephant groan, as if saying, 'so, this is Sicily, OK, now get me some decent clean petrol!'

Our plan was, as always, simple. We would get Elephant serviced in Sicily, ride east and get to Greece, then turn north and head for Finland. Back in the land of digital mapping, we had programmed the GPS well in advance with the location of the BMW dealer but, unfortunately, not the BMW *moto* dealer. After checking out the new BMW cars, it took us another hour in the traffic to find the *moto* place. It was, we rationalised, time well spent getting used to local traffic. The Sicilian drivers, we quickly decided, made the Italians look like masters of restraint.

We weren't surprised when the BMW dealer couldn't service Elephant late on Friday afternoon, but the friendly and helpful service manager booked us in for Monday and gave us the address of a business to fix a slow leak that had started in our rear tyre a couple of weeks before. We were told to ask for Mario Gambino and we did just that when we arrived at the tyre place an hour later.

Mario had been phoned and told that we were on our way. He and his team marvelled at the Elephant's fit-out, where we had been, where we were planning to go, and the whole idea of the Ulysses Club and its crazy motto. In short order, they removed a shard of steel from the tyre, repaired the wound, and pumped it with 3.5 bar of Palermo smog.

I asked how much I owed him but Mario just shrugged his shoulders, spread his arms in a welcoming gesture, and said something we took to mean 'welcome to Sicily!' Then he invited us to have lunch with him at the newly opened restaurant next door.

The restaurant's proprietor, Antonio, had learned his trade during 17 years in New York and had returned with his family to make a big investment in his hometown. We had the best pizza we'd had since New York, exchanged stories about our families, and enjoyed the first Italian coffee we'd had for a while. We left Mario with a Ulysses sticker, still chuckling over Antonio's translation of the Ulysses motto: 'Grow Old Disgracefully'; and the special club handshake we had shown him. With two days to explore western Sicily, we headed for the coastal town of Trapani, a warm hotel, two more alarmingly good pizzas, and a longneck of local beer.

By the time the Elephant was back from the BMW dealership three days later, we had discovered that Sicily was full of challenging mountain roads and ancient villages clumped precariously on the top of the hills. We walked all over Palermo from our hotel in a less salubrious quarter, ate some great Sicilian food, and started to get used to the budgetary reality of being back in Euro-land.

The Elephant was also in good fettle with new fuel filters after the lousy petrol in North Africa and new rear brake pads. The warranty, which had been our saviour in Spain, had expired the day after the service.

We set out for Messina on the eastern coast by the old coastal road. The 250 kilometres took more than 8 hours in the saddle and was a good explanation for the construction of the *autostrada*. The road wound a tortured path through the hilly coastal terrain with villages huddled over the narrow track and jutting their sharp edges into blind corners facing more blind corners. After four hours and a dozen close misses, the picturesque became grotesque.

We started to wonder what the builders of this giant rabbit warren were thinking as we ground out the day to Messina. We rolled into town with some relief and elected to stay overnight but even this decision seemed designed to frustrate us. We struggled to find a hotel, parking and food and we were pleased to see the city disappear in our wake as the ferry pulled away the next morning.

After the ferry from Sicily to Italy, it was an easy decision to select a combination of *autostrada* and back roads for the ride across the bottom of Italy to Brindisi on the east coast. We rolled along through the open farmland at a comfortable pace and had a much more satisfactory overnight stop at the old Mediterranean naval town of Taranto.

The early buds were starting to show on the fruit trees lined up in their regimental rows, espaliered flat to simplify the husbandry. Everywhere the first tentative flush of the Mediterranean spring poked up to meet a sun that was still weak and a wind that cut across the plain as a reminder that the mountains and the snow were still not far away.

Brindisi was an interesting town at the end of the Appian Way that had been the step off point for the Crusaders on their way to the Holy Land. As soon as we arrived we bought tickets for the only ferry running to Igoumenitsa, Greece, departing at 7pm then spent a few hours seeing the sights. We were starting to get used to these Mediterranean ferries so we got ourselves down to the docks late enough to ensure we were last on and close to the loading ramp. We secured Elephant with a single strap across the seat and the machine resting on its sidestand. We had found that this was the easiest and most secure way of keeping everything in place. Other riders seemed to strap their machines upright with tension on the suspension from straps left and right. While this worked OK if the straps didn't loosen, it was harder to execute, required two straps instead of one and caused the bike to fall if a strap failed. A loose strap with our system left the bike on its sidestand, which was still reasonably secure.

With Elephant secured, we adjourned to the bar and spent the 8-hour passage chatting with an English couple on their way to Greece to spy out a permanent mooring for their yacht. The husband, Steve, had once ridden a 250cc two-stroke Harley Davidson (who remembers this desperate period of Harley history these days?) through Algeria and across the Sahara to Mali and had some great stories to tell about that adventure so the time went quickly. As we pulled into port, the truck drivers who had been whiling away the time watching videos scrambled for their vehicles and we wished our companions good luck and went looking for Elephant.

With a reliability matched by little else around the Med, it had started to rain heavily several hours before we rumbled down the ramp at 4am Greek time into a port town with nothing open. If we had a rush of enthusiasm as we stormed past the semis up a new freeway heading into the night then it only lasted for as long as the new road, about 25 kilometres. After that it was down to business and we hustled east halfway across the width of the country and then south along the twisting mountain road through the dark.

Unfortunately, the headlights on Elephant were a hopeless disgrace. I cursed myself that I had not organised an upgrade and promised to do so before our next night ride. The road wound high into the mountains through slumbering villages and misty gorges; slippery in the wet and full of surprising, tightening-radius turns. Although we hadn't slept for 24 hours, there was enough fear abroad in the night to keep us both wide awake.

I had Kylie on and, while she was of little extra value in navigation, she proved a blessing for the ride. With the heavy rain and poor headlights, hairpin bends were coming out of the dark at us at an alarming rate. By adjusting the scale of the screen and zooming in on the road, I could make the bends appear on the screen before they appeared in the lights and see how tight the turn was likely to be. Despite this, we were reduced to a crawl and several big semis from the ferry, equipped with enough lights to power a small city, eventually caught and passed us.

By dawn it was still raining and cold, but we were thankful for the light and just hustled on. We stopped for fuel and breakfast too early to get anything hot to eat, then pressed on again into a grey low-cloud day. By midday we were half way down the country and it was late enough for us to find a hotel. We turned off the main road bypass and found a warm and comfortable room in the prosperous town of Messolongi.

An hour later we were in warm dry clothes with our bellies full of moussaka and beans. We were tired, but we had the feeling that we had done a pretty good night's work. It was the first time we had been to Greece for about 20 years but we still had great memories of the wonderful month we spent here with Sarah and Nick in 1990. It was good to be back.

A lot had changed since our last visit to Greece. The country we remembered was a bit of a backwater, friendly, quaint and a little clunky. The country we found has been transformed by its membership of the EU and cheap money. The place looked and felt prosperous, it had the beginning of a cosmopolitan culture (albeit one with central European bent), and all of the usual problems of an awakening Western market economy. Of course, the new economy and the cheap money hadn't reached all, or even most of the people. The complaints we heard, about the young losing respect for the 'old ways'; and the insidiousness of US pop culture, sounded very familiar.

The Greeks were not fully used to the new face of their country. In one coffee shop, over a poor Greek imitation of an Italian coffee, a prosperous looking businessman in an overstuffed shirt explained that the newcomers brought discrimination on themselves because they dressed and acted differently. We bit our tongues and said nothing. We were visitors and felt it better to stay off the moral high ground. We had both heard the same type of remark about Moslem immigrants to Australia in recent times, and Vietnamese, Chinese, Italian and even Greek migrants in the past. The one thing that the Greeks could learn from New World countries is that the anger would pass, but there would be pain along the way.

The great news for our journey, however, was that all of the things we loved on our last visit were still there, even if the prices were now in Euros and that much more expensive. The food was great, the people straight-forward, and the country still rugged and beautiful.

We arrived in Greece on the Friday of a long weekend for the celebration of Shrove Monday, also known as Clean Monday. As we rode into Athens on the Saturday morning, a river of traffic flowed in the opposite direction out of the city. We had wondered why the huge and almost empty hotel in Messolonghi had had no rooms for the Saturday. We saw the reason pouring past us: a torrent of cars leaving for the provinces.

The Sunday of the long weekend was marked by a *carnivale* with big street parades. While the Brazilians were probably not in danger of losing their crown for hosting the ultimate street party, the Greeks did a great job of parading in the streets dressed in silly costumes and eating and drinking far too much. All of this in the name of piety, mind you.

We spent the weekend in Athens, staying in an area inhabited mainly by Romanians (don't ask us). The unexpected upside of our visit was that the air, having been cleaned with recent snow and the Friday's rain, remained as clear as crystal as the usual polluters spread their vehicle exhausts further afield for three days. We put on our walking shoes (our only shoes) and made the best of the brilliant, warm spring weather and the clean air in this usually smoggy city.

Our reason for coming to Athens was to resolve some problems with our visas for Russia. We had departed London without a full solution to our problem, but the folk at the Russian Consulate had been most helpful, and had told us we could get our visas in Budapest. Stupidly, we had been encouraged by this. Getting visas for Russia was the sort of administrative nightmare that ensured that only the determined travel there independently.

To start with, we were still 2400 kilometres and seven countries away from our entry point into Russia and it would take us up to 60 days to get there. Our target entry date was 1 June. To get a visa, we needed an invitation from an organisation inside Russia. This is the same for all visas but because we needed a visa for three months (it's a big place) and for multiple entries (we wanted to go to Kazakhstan and Mongolia as well), we had to have a business visa.

The problem was that the organisation that was inviting us couldn't apply for our invitation from the relevant ministry until 45 days prior to our entry date. It would then take 18 days to process our invitation request. The original copy of the invitation would need to be delivered to us and we could then apply for a visa at a Russian Consulate. The consulates all operated separately, and had different rules depending on the host countries, but they all had a rule forbidding them from issuing visas to third-party nationals. That is, the Greek Consulate could only issue visas to Greeks or those with Greek residency. All others had to make application in their country of residence. Once we did find a consul to process the application, the administration would take 10 days and in the end, there was no guarantee that we would be granted the visa we needed for the trip we wanted to do.

Notwithstanding the rules, the Russian Consul in Athens assured us that she would process our visas in Athens and gave us some hope that the Hungarian Russians might do the same. In light of all this we reorganised our disorganised plan and decided to try to process our visas at the Consulate in Budapest in early May. This would allow us to make application inside the 45-day limit and be close enough to get to the border in the time between granting the visa and its start date. We also decided that solving these problems on the road was a sure-fire way to stave off Alzheimer's, if nothing else.

From Athens we headed south into the Peloponnese, that large southern protrusion joined to the mainland by a thin isthmus at Corinth. This is where you can find Sparta, Olympia, Kalamata and the village of Githio where Paris took some folk dancing lessons from Helen before stealing her away to Troy and starting a war. In the Peloponnese we also found those idyllic Mediterranean scenes with crystal clear water and beautiful villages that we associate with the Greek Islands. Here, however, we didn't have to travel by another ferry. Instead, we rode through the rugged mountains over some of the most spectacular bike roads and enjoyed the spring weather with Elephant.

Having survived big-city Greece in Athens, we were pleased to settle into the gentle routine of the southern coast. Our days developed a rhythm of late starts, careful rides over treacherous mountain roads and lazy evenings wandering picturesque villages. Interspersed with this was the constant round of hunting and gathering to keep us accommodated, fed and healthy on the road. We found that rooms for rent were cheaper and often more comfortable than hotels, many had wonderful outlooks and communal kitchen facilities that allowed us to make our own breakfast.

These were days of idyll as we wandered down the coast of the Peloponnese and sauntered through that series of thin peninsulas which jut into the Mediterranean and on to the towns of Monemvasia, Githio and Koroni, stopping for picnic lunches in olive groves and by picturesque harbours. One great feature of Greece was that we usually found a place by the road to make tea and eat our cheese, bread and olives. The small mountaineering stove we carried was put into service several times a day.

Our first week ended in the small tourist village of Nafplio. At a taverna full of locals, we had a very traditional Greek meal of salad, grilled fish and octopus. We ate the same meal often during our last visit. This time, however, we walked a few blocks to an ice cream shop and wandered home licking a superb if expensive chocolate and chilli gelato. Welcome to Euro-Greece!

Spring weather was on the way and the weather was mostly dry and good for riding. Buoyed by the warm days, we enjoyed the sort of relaxed week you would expect in a country where we knew the way things worked and how to make ourselves at home. We also found that many of the roads in this part of Greece were both challenging and exhilarating. The country itself was rugged and beautiful but without the breathtaking drama of the mountains in Morocco. The upside was the perfect scenes that greeted us at every stop along the coast.

With rugged mountains plunging straight into the sea, it was like riding your favourite bike road every day without rounding the same corner twice. Some of it was challenging. West of Sparta the mountain road clambered up through dozens of impossible switchbacks but, with the long winter in the Moroccan mountains behind us, Elephant's hairpin technique was close to faultless. We found ourselves swaying through the hills as though we were performing a kind of swooping dance; a mechanical ballet with an Elephant in a tutu.

We spent hours riding in first, second and third gear (we had 6) entering the corners wide and deep, turning late and hard only when I could see the exit then keeping plenty of power going to the back wheel to keep it planted firmly (you have to think about the physics sometimes). This is the classic bike cornering technique designed to give the rider options and traction and to keep the bike coming out of the corners on the safe side of the road. Failure to master this simple method has killed more good men and women than the plague.

All riders learn, or should learn, this technique when they are trained and most riders practise it to some degree. We relied on it, however, as our first trick for survival. Occasionally, we judged a corner wrong and Elephant ran a little wide or a little tight or we found ourselves in the wrong gear for the exit but no transgression was allowed to pass without critique and each one was a reminder that elephants aren't human, but Elephant riders are.

On our way north we visited Olympia. We had been there with

Sarah and Nick and we had no desire to see the archaeological site again. We did, however, have two pressing reasons to go there. Firstly, we needed to buy a postcard from Olympia for our friends Bob and Jenny Cook, whose daughter Sarah had just been selected for the Olympic Rowing Team, and it didn't seem right to buy one anywhere else but Olympia. The second reason was to see the new Museum of the Modern Olympics, which had not been there for our last visit.

The postcard was no problem. The museum turned into a Greek joke. We had noted that there was industrial trouble in the air during our time in Athens (the riot police gathering near our hotel was a dead give-away) and we knew the garbage collectors were out because of the mountains of uncollected rubbish in every village. We then found out that the postal workers were on strike when we tried to buy a stamp for the Cook's card. The penny finally dropped and we realised that the whole of the public service was up in arms when the museum was closed because of the strike action. In the end we found a stamp in a tourist shop and dutifully dropped the card in the box at the post office. We discovered much later that the card was never delivered. Obviously the New Greece hadn't quite made it to the public services stage.

It took us more than an hour to find the right road out of Olympia and into the mountains to the north-east. I'm still not sure what navigation glitch caused this confusion, but some days can be like that. As it turned out, it was an hour we would have appreciated later in the day. The 250-kilometre run to Kalavrita took us all day on the tortured mountain roads. We realised early on that it was going to be a long day but we still stuck to our routine of regular meal and travel breaks and took an hour out to visit the limestone caves at Limnon.

Jo was very keen to see these as they are reputed to be some of the best in the world, made special by a series of cascading lakes within the caves. The caves were interesting enough but, unfortunately, the cascading lakes were mainly dry. Our theory was that the guy who turns on the water for the lakes was on strike. The guide claimed that the lake-less condition of the caves was due to poor snow during the winter, but we knew industrial action when we saw it!

North from the Limnon Caves, the village of Kalavrita was a ski resort. This made it high, cold and expensive, all of which are good reasons not to take a bike there. To add to the silliness, we spent an hour freezing on a park bench next to an expensive hotel to use some free WiFi and get some emails done.

The town itself was full of modern boutiques with expensive ski gear and expensive bars largely deserted at the end of the season. All of this was out of our price range but we managed to find a traditional local eatery in an older part of town and enjoyed a hearty meal and a bottle of local wine. There was a light dusting of snow as we wandered back to our digs.

From Kalavrita our spring weather deserted us for a day for the ride over the mountains to Patra, and the bridge from the Peloponnese to the mainland. But by the time we were heading up the Ionian Coast towards the island of Lefkada, the skies were clear and we were stripping off excess gear again.

We first heard of the island of Lefkada on our trip over from Brindisi from a couple of English sailors who were intending to buy a mooring there. A permanent base in Lefkada would, they reasoned, be warmer and cheaper than their UK base. We arrived at Lefkada to find that many others had the same idea. Hundreds of yachts were laid up for winter near the town, while many others filled the marinas in the main town and the many small harbours around the island. It didn't take us long to work out why yachties loved the place. The water was clean, warm and sheltered and the villages were lively.

We circled the island then settled down for a few days at the town of Nidri where we found another room with a wonderful view. Nidri was a second or third tier tourist town with cheaper accommodation and a handful of cafés and bars cluttered along the waterfront. It was a place for yatchies and there were protected moorings and small slipways all along a section of narrow estuary. Many boats were pulled up for the winter for maintenance or parked on frames in makeshift boat parks. The place had that smell of rotting seaweed and salt that I always associated with boyhood holidays at my grandparents' house on the old industrial waterfront at Balmain on Sydney Harbour.

A few days at Nidri gave us a chance to catch up on some make and mend and wash our riding suits. Since we had been wearing them most days for more than six months, the suits were so filthy that we joked that they walked around on their own and just took us along for the ride. They stank and turned a bath full of warm soapy water dark brown!

We liked our little Greek off-season seaside village very much and would have stayed on for a few more days except the apartment complex we stayed at did not have any rooms with a double bed. Now call me old fashioned, but three days of struggling with the bedding on two singles pushed together was enough.

We were also worried about some very bad weather that was chilling Northern Europe and heading south. Each night we watched the weather reports on Greek television and calculated how the cold would affect us when it moved south. We decided that our best bet to stay dry was on the east coast and that the quickest way there was straight over the mountains through the town of Karpenissi.

We reasoned that we only needed one day to relocate to the other side of the country 340 kilometres away and elected to make a run for it while the weather held. All it took for us to make this silly decision was a few days of balmy spring weather and short memories. Sometimes you can bring a curse on yourself by the simplest things.

The morning of Monday 24 March, we held off departure until 10.30am to check on the weather. It looked good. We paid our bill, said goodbye to our landlord and headed for the hills. By the time we were charging across the causeway to the mainland 40 minutes later the blasting cross winds hit us and we were wondering about the wisdom of our decision. By the time we reached the foothills two hours later we had our rain-suits on, and by the time we reached the mountains three hours later we knew it was going to be a long day.

I have never minded riding in the rain, or riding in gusty cross-winds, or riding challenging mountain roads, but all three together is different matter. The road twisted itself into a tortured knot of switchback corners and the rain thundered down turning the hairpins into rivers and covering them in debris. The lightning seemed to strike on top of us and the thunder hit us with a wave of energy that shook us to the core. We climbed on. The storm wind ripped down the valleys and hit Elephant with a hammer-blow each time we were exposed from the lee of a spur.

High in the mountains it started to hail. Big clumps of ice smashed into our helmets and arms and Elephant struggled to keep a steady grip on the marble road. My arms and shoulders started to ache and I realised that I was gripping the controls too tightly trying to make each input smooth. I tried to relax by shaking my shoulders consciously to release the knotted muscles and I found myself talking to Elephant, murmuring soothing, cooing sounds, steadying nerves.

We pushed on with nowhere to stop and nowhere to hide. Occasionally we closed on and passed a car or bus on the torturous road, but mostly we felt alone and exposed on the mountain. The only town of any size on our route was Karpenissi. The 240 kilometres to get there took 6 hours in the saddle and by the time we creaked into town we were chilled to the bone and running out of light. The temperature was 0^0C and falling quickly. It was an easy decision to call an end to the day's ride and look for shelter.

We were in luck and it didn't take long to find a deliciously warm hotel that was only a little over our budget, not that we were in a quibbling mood. We lugged our gear inside and within minutes had changed into dry clothes and struggled back onto the street a little warmer in our down jackets. A few yards down the hill we found a bottle of very good Shiraz/Grenâche and some tolerably good take-away. We hurried back to the room and gulped down our hot food and warming wine curled up safe and warm in bed. It had been a hell of a day at the office.

Tuesday 25 March is Greek Independence Day and a public holiday. We set the alarm early and opened the window to an amazing sight. It was snowing! Even Elephant had a light covering. We waited. It kept snowing. At 10am we told the hotel we were staying and settled in to read novels and watch some Greek TV. At 3pm Karpenissi appeared on the afternoon news covered in its blanket of newsworthy, unseasonable snow. The shot showed the main street where our hotel was located and there, in the corner of the screen, parked on the footpath, was Elephant with a thick pad of snow on its cosy grey cover!

That night the snow turned to rain and it thundered down without stop until the early morning. We had a fitful night's sleep waking to look out at the rain each hour or so but by break of dawn the sky started to clear. By the time we were packed to ride at 9am, the mountains around the town looked magnificent in the clear morning light. But we weren't waiting around to enjoy the view.

We tumbled down the mountain. In 20 minutes we were below the snow line and the road was drying. In 40 minutes we were on the coastal plain heading for the town of Lamia. We turned south and flogged Elephant down the motorway to Athens. We needed to do some important administration towards getting our Russian visas and Athens was the best place to get it sorted.

We booked into the same hotel we had stayed at on our last visit, the Pergamos. The hotel itself had nothing much to recommend it above the other tourist-class places in the area except that the front desk was manned by Stefanos, who is a former teacher of politics and history. Stefanos was a walking encyclopaedia on matters of Greek culture, history and politics, and was worth the tariff and the simple breakfast just to have him there to answer our questions. We didn't even mind staying an extra day when the weather closed in with heavy rain in this notoriously dry city.

On the morning of 29 March, with as much done towards a Russian visa as we could manage, we left Athens and pushed 450 kilometres north to the east coast area that the weather forecasts assured us would be sunny. We stopped at the town of Platamonas. It was not much different to a dozen other touristy settlements along this part of the coast except that we had stayed there with

Sarah and Nick. We walked up to the same castle we had walked to all those years ago and took some photos. The castle hadn't changed but it now cost €2 to get in. Last time the only person there was the local goat herder.

We remembered a sleepy village with a couple of tavernas where fresh fish was always on the grill. What we found was a pedestrianised street and a dozen glitzy bars, coffee shops and restaurants. While we strolled along the waterfront a private helicopter landed in front of one of the restaurants and the occupants disappeared inside. The new Platamonas was probably a good end point for our visit to Greece. Much of what we loved about Greece was still there and it was still a country where we felt completely at home. However, the new Greece was also a modern country on the move, with plenty of swagger and self-confidence, as well as all the problems and doubts that plague the rest of the modern world.

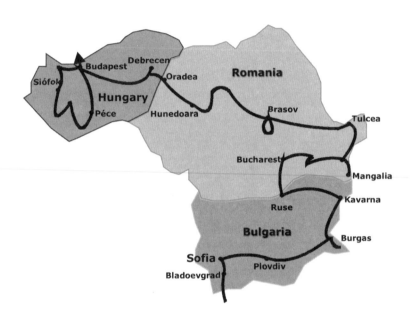

9

Central Europe

Lots of stuff closes down on Sunday in Greece so we had a difficult time finding an open fuel station in the north of the country while trying to stay clear of the main towns. After running the tank down just short of the reserve, we headed for Thessalonika (the nearest big town) to find some fuel. When we finally located a station, we had only pumped 10 litres into the tank before the power blacked out and the pump stopped. We took this as an omen and so closed in on the border at Lefkonas to overnight, ready to get out of Greece the next day.

The Bulgarian border was easy. We didn't get off the bike and we were through in a few minutes. The longest part of the proceedings was a short conversation with the immigration man about how far we had come on the bike and where we wanted to go. He sent us on our way with a good luck wish and a big smile and that pretty much set the tone for our first week in Bulgaria.

Bulgaria got itself free from the Ottoman Empire in the late 19th century but unfortunately only had a few years of independence before falling into the orbit of a Soviet Russia. The following 70-year hibernation left the country poor and underdeveloped. In the last 15 years, the country has pulled itself into the modern age, with the pace of change accelerating over the last five as the country gained EU membership. Not that this membership has been without controversy. Other EU members openly expressed the view that there was too much corruption and poor governance in Bulgaria for it to be a full member. Within the country there were also some misgivings.

Now that we were in a former Soviet Block country, we started to speak to locals who pined for the old days of the Soviet Union when everyone had a job and no one worked too hard because there was no way to get ahead by working hard. At first we listened politely and even sympathised a little, but after a while our patience with this constant complaint wore thin. I developed a rather sardonic line of response that went along the lines of, 'Welcome to our world!', which I'd follow up with pithy observations pointing out that if Bulgarians (insert Romanians or others here) wanted to succeed in the West, then harder work, and better quality work, were needed in most areas of life. The slipshod standards of the communist days would not do.

Much of the social lethargy, however, could be traced back to the levels of corruption evident in everyday life and it was this that seemed to underpin a sense of helplessness among the ordinary people. 'What can we do?', they would often say with a shrug.

There was still plenty of poverty in Bulgaria, particularly in the rural areas where a new economy was yet to get moving, but much of the country was starting to express the first signs of a new prosperity. We rode north into a changing landscape; greener, wetter and, unfortunately, colder and stopped in the regional centre of Blagoevgrad. We found a warm room in a hotel in the industrial outskirts then walked the town getting used to a new place and new people.

In Blagoevgrad, as in other centres, good use had been made

of the open public spaces left over from the Soviet period. A strong café culture had developed with many smart restaurants and coffee shops looking strangely out of place against the huge Soviet era monuments that remained as silent sentries watching over each square. Still, the monolithic soviet architecture at least gave the city a sense of order and space and the regiments of characterless apartment blocks were still a practical means to keep the population off the streets both literally and figuratively.

Further to the north, we drifted into the capital city of Sofia, a city of about 1.5 million souls that did a good impression of a laid-back, comfortable sort of place. Its architecture showed a distinct Russian influence but was well-proportioned and attractive. We liked the look of the place and felt that, in general, it lacked the bombast of some western cities. The historic sites were another matter. After the wonderful sites of North Africa the historic landscape this was all a little ho-hum. We did the rounds on foot and got some useful exercise but little of the history of the place was accessible.

Of more interest was the early discovery that Bulgarian beer is great and the local Traminer, Chardonnay, and Cabernet Sauvignon were all good enough and keenly priced. This was one area of the economy of each country in which we took a keen interest and started to develop a sort of comparative well-being index. One evening I pontificated that a country with lousy beer and no wine industry to mention would score very low on the index and should receive aid from the better well-being- endowed countries.

On this score, Bulgaria should have been sending their brewers to help breweries world wide to raise their game while the Bulgarians should be the recipients of wine-aid to push their winemaking up to competitive levels. This seemed reasonable enough until Jo asked about those countries without decent beer *or* wine. These unfortunates, we decided, should get a special UN package of assistance managed by UNESCO.

Bulgarian traffic was well ordered in a way that we hadn't seen in any of the Mediterranean countries or North Africa. In the big cities of Sofia and Plovdiv, however, many of the streets were cobbled and in Sofia the cobbles came with both tram tracks and rain, neither of which were good fun. Down one tight Plovdiv lane I tried to turn the bike in its own length and had what we politely call a 'static drop'. The front wheel had dropped into a hole and with no forward momentum, the wheel had slapped over to full lock and we were down in a second. Elephant spilled both of us onto the road in front of the large window of a printing business. After the mandatory check that we were both uninjured, we had the problem of standing up Elephant, luggage and all. As I positioned myself to make the lift, Jo started to pull on part of the bike in an attempt to help. She was clearly a little upset after the shock of the fall. I had to stop and firmly insist that she step back and leave the job to me. This was not macho posturing. Jo had still not fully recovered from her back injury and there was every chance she would injure herself struggling with 300kg of Elephant and luggage. There is a technique for lifting big bikes and I had had plenty of experience with over the years. I got myself into position down at the lower side of the handlebars and, with arms and back straight, rose and hauled Elephant upright. Once Elephant was up, Jo got the sidestand down and the job was done. My heart was pounding and tension-sweat ran down my back when I noticed that the audience watching from the nearby window were clearly surprised that the big machine was righted. It was then I looked up and there, standing by his van, was the driver who had blocked our way. He was waiting for us to right the beast so that he could continue on his route.

In view of his lack of practical assistance, I took my time to get back into the saddle and to get Jo comfortable behind me then I rolled forward until my front wheel was close to his front bumper then waved him to move with a dismissive flick of my left hand. He pointed to the space beside the van indicating that I should go around. I repeated the 'get out of the way' gesture. He looked at us for a few seconds summing up his options and no doubt worked out that it was not a good idea to argue with an angry man wearing a helmet, an armoured suit and padded gloves. He climbed into the van and backed into open space in the square behind while we rolled past. There was no doubt Team Elephant was toughening up.

We enjoyed the old city of Plovdiv which was being renovated to preserve some important Bulgarian history. The city had been the centre for the National Revival Period beginning early in the 19th Century and culminating in liberation from Turkey in 1878. Some houses that reflected the architecture of this period, and held historical collections celebrating the significant development of the nationalist movement, had been restored and opened to the public. Others had been turned into restaurants or apartments. The overall effect was pleasing in a clean, safe and cheerful way, and we enjoyed wandering the city and exploring the back streets.

We had planned to spend two days in Plovdiv, but early on the second day it started raining and it kept on raining for the next 48 hours. Despite our hotel room being slightly smaller than a shoe box, we settled in to watch cable TV, read and wait. We ventured down to the bar only for beer and braved the weather outside only to eat.

On our third night we decided that we would head to the Black Sea coast the next day, rain or no, and went to bed listening to the steady beat of the storm against the window. I slept fitfully, waking every hour or so and looking out to see heavy, consistent rain,. Sometime not long before dawn, however, the rain cleared and we woke to crystal skies and an icy wind that was slowly drying the roads. Seeing our chance, we bolted.

The road to the Black Sea coast ran across the black soil of the Thracian Plain. This expanse of fertile flatlands covered one third of Bulgaria and ran north to the border and the Danube River Delta. It also explained the historic wealth of these lands and why Thracian wines were world famous before the Romans had introduced grapes to the Gauls. We rolled through the major coastal city of Burgas and cruised south into the little coastal town of Sozopol in the early afternoon. It started to rain shortly after but we were home and dry.

For the next two days we explored the 200 kilometres that constitutes the Bulgarian Black Sea coast. The first thing we noticed was that we were asked routinely if we were visiting to buy an apartment or land. There are real estate agents everywhere specialising in selling property to Western Europeans.

One evening we were the only customers in a tiny restaurant and struck up a conversation with the owner. He asked where we came from and, inevitably, if we were there looking for an apartment. We laughed spontaneously then, fearing we might have hurt his feelings, explained that we lived on a beautiful coast and didn't think we needed a second place on the Bulgarian Black Sea.

'Ah,' he said, 'but this coast is very beautiful.'

'Yes it is,' I lied, while Jo busied herself with some detail of her salad.

The conversation went on like this for a few minutes until I asked him if he had internet access. When he confirmed that he had a connected computer in his office, I gave him the net address of a Gold Coast web site. This site had no information. It was simply a camera that continually swept one of the important surfing beaches so that you could get up in the morning, check the conditions, and decide if you would go to work or go surfing. I had always thought of this as elegant in an antipodean sort of way.

Later, when we had finished our meal and were washing away the last of our day with the last of our wine, he came back in with a big grin of understanding on his face. He had looked up the net address and seen the beach by moonlight with people walking in the sand and a perfect shore break running white pencil lines across the scene.

We wandered out into the chill night air with belly laughs all round and on the way back to our digs started to wonder how much longer we would be riding in the cool weather. It seemed that every time it got a little warmer, we headed north again to press up against the edge of winter. Our dinner conversation about our Queensland home had left us wishing for the simplicity of riding in a milder climate.

By the time of our visit in early April 2008, most of the Bulgarian Black Sea coast was a construction site. Huge villa and resort developments were underway to satisfy the appetite of those poor British or Germans who missed the cheap deals in Spain and wanted a cheap place in the sun. For about £150,000 you too could buy a three-bedroom apartment on a hill some distance from the sea but with a sea view. It was awful. The further up the coast we rode the more depressed we became. Soon there would be nothing left but soulless concrete condominiums.

In our explorations down back roads (oh, the joys of being an independent traveller!) we found two old overgrown holiday camps dating back to the communist days. We rode around the barricades and signs that blocked entry and idled along pathways overgrown with grass and vines. They had the look of military camps with low-set huts and communal facilities. The buildings had been cheaply built and were now falling down. The forest was slowly claiming back its own and actively lifting and pushing the old huts aside.

The camps were almost laughable compared with the huge resort developments just a few kilometres up the coast, but as we talked about our discovery we realised that our best family holidays had never been in resorts. It seemed to us that most families were like ours and could have as memorable a holiday camping, or at Comrade Butlins, as they could at the Ramada Black Sea Resort. The problem with all the new developments was that they were swallowing the whole of the coast. Soon there would be nothing left that was not the exclusive preserve of a hotel, condominium or resort.

In the end we were too depressed by all of this to stay on the coast. We had no doubt that this would all end badly for the Bulgarians. Between boorish Westerners and corrupt local officials the whole of the coast would soon be alienated from the ordinary people and Bulgaria would be poorer for it. We did the only thing we could do and headed north-west away from the coast, back into the rural heartland to close up on the Danube River.

After a ride halfway across the country (not so far really) we reached the Danube and the Bulgarian frontier at the town of Ruse. We took a room on the 13th floor of an old Soviet era hotel that was ridiculously expensive and falling apart. It did, however, give us a wonderful view over the city, the river and the port.

We spent our last day in Bulgaria wandering around the old city while I snapped photos of some of the old Soviet era cars that were still on the roads. Bulgaria had been a pleasant surprise for us. Despite the difficult language and Cyrillic script, we were very comfortable there. The people were genuinely friendly and pleased that we were not just there to buy a cheap apartment. The wine was fine, the beer was great, and we fed ourselves well and often. In one sense it was a good result all round. In another, it left us unsettled.

For us, the most telling comparison in Bulgaria was not between city wealth and rural poverty, as it had been in other developing countries, but between the cities with their ample and well ordered Soviet-era parks and public spaces; and the coastal areas where rampant development would soon alienate the entire coastline from the Bulgarian people. A stifling communist administration never had much to recommend it, but neither did the unfettered development then underway. We were learning that the travellers' prerogative of being a critical observer sometimes brought with it the pain of being witness to folly.

We crossed into Romania over the wide Danube River on 10 April and rolled north towards the capital. Romania was another small country and, with more than 20 million people, it had a high population density and a generally crowded feel. As soon as we rode over the border we found ourselves in heavily congested traffic on the main road heading north to the capital, Bucharest. We had found a list of Bucharest hotels on the web and had good mapping of the city for the GPS so we anticipated a relatively easy run into this big city. By the time we closed in on the city centre, however, the traffic was nearly gridlocked and the Elephant was an overheated handful.

After an hour and a half in the crawling traffic to check five hotels, we settled on a place that offered a 20 percent discount because it was undergoing renovation. It was still too expensive, at €52 per night, and was located on a main square in front of the railway station, making it the noisiest hotel we had stayed in for many years. We ditched our gear, changed into our walking shoes and got to know the place in the best possible way; by walking all over it.

After two days of walking from one end of town to the other our feelings about Bucharest were mixed. On one level it was a very beautiful city. It was remodelled in the 19th Century by French architects and had some wonderful buildings and world-class parks, but it also had appalling traffic congestion that left most of the city gridlocked much of the day. This was another city that the cars ate.

With that wonderful clarity of the outsider who sees little, understands nothing and has opinions on everything, we had developed a measure of city live-ability based on the degree to which people and vehicles were separated. Under our scheme, where vehicles are allowed to invade the space for people, the amenity of the city was seriously eroded. On this scale, Bucharest got points for parks which were large, plentiful, well designed and maintained, but lost points for allowing vehicles to park anywhere and drive almost anywhere.

Bucharest also got a big tick for having water features that worked. We had seen dozens of water features on our travels and almost all were under repair and dry! Bucharest managed hectares of fountains all blasting water into the spring air.

We liked Bucharest but it was 'Western European-expensive' so after two days of being kept awake by the Railway Square traffic, we packed up and rode east to another Black Sea coast. This was mostly an uneventful ride over the broad plains of the Danube valley, that is, after we had spent an hour and a half getting out of town in the Saturday morning gridlock. By the time we cleared the city the engine was overheated and was detonating under load. The rider was just detonating.

We found a room at an inexpensive, empty resort hotel in the town of Mangalia. Jo felt a little unwell the next morning so we decided to stay and have a quiet time while we wandered around this seedy old holiday town. That evening Jo had only fruit to eat while I chanced my arm with a local kebab from the only take away place doing a good trade. It was a bad mistake. Although I woke feeling fine the following morning, by early afternoon I knew that I had eaten contaminated food. The stomach cramps were almost bending me in two.

The day was also eventful in other ways. During the two days, the Elephant sat in the hotel's front garden under its cover. Unfortunately it also sat with its parking lights on as I had inadvertently turned the key one click too far before removal. It was a silly mistake that left our battery so flat it wouldn't run the GPS much less spark the ignition.

As has often happened in tight situations, a friendly local went out of his way to assist us. A delivery driver was having coffee when I went back into the hotel. He brought his van around and parked in close. We didn't have a set of jumper cables, but we found two lengths of 10 amp electrical cable. From (bitter) experience I knew that these would not provide the power to crank the engine so we connected the cables and let the Elephant draw some power from the van for about 15 minutes, resisting the temptation to press the starter and smoke the cables. When there was enough power in Elephant's battery to give a bright ignition light, we unloaded the luggage and Jo and the van-man gave a big, running push while I jump-started the beast in 3rd gear. The engine fired easily and we were away!

Although I kicked myself for leaving the lights on, this incident gave me a little more confidence that between us we had the capacity to solve the problems that lay in wait and that we would get ourselves and Elephant through to Vladivostok. Elephant offered no opinion but I felt sure confidence was growing all round.

After such a bad start we rode the length of the Romanian Black Sea coast to the town of Tulcea on the edge of the Danube Delta arriving in our rain suits with Elephant caked in mud thrown up on the dirty road. We had three days on the Delta. Ostensibly, one day to see the sights and two to wait for the rain to stop but, in reality, three days to decide if I could ride with my deteriorating health.

We did manage to see something of the Danube Delta, which is a huge World Heritage listed wetland, but mucking around in swamps in the rain holds limited interest when you are feeling ill. By the second day I was concerned that I had more than the usual traveller's diarrhoea. The symptoms weren't quite right and it had persisted for longer than was usual with me (I had always been very robust in this department). I checked our medical book and took a course of antibiotics from our drug kit and, although I was feeling very fragile, on the first fine morning we decided to head back to the centre of the country in search of dry weather.

By the time we got to Brasov 380 kilometres away I was seriously ill and sure that the medication I had taken had not worked. Apart from the direct symptoms, I was running out of energy from missing meals and dehydrating as the diarrhoea took the fluids straight out of me. Riding all day in this condition was very hard. I gave Jo a brief commentary on my condition but kept my own counsel on how worried I was about its possible outcome.

Following the advice of our medical books I had worked out what I didn't have, leaving amoebic dysentery as the most likely culprit. We were carrying the right drugs to treat the amoeba but had only one third of the needed quantity. I took the drugs I had immediately and went looking for more. By the next day I was showing a slight improvement and had found more of the necessary drugs. By day two of the treatment the symptoms had disappeared completely and I was sure I had nailed it. Though physically drained, I felt well and morale was mostly mended by the time we rolled out of Brasov on the morning of 20 April.

Travelling west from Brasov, we found the Transylvania Highway and, eventually, Transylvania. Jo kept the clove of garlic she had been saving in the food box readily at hand. Vampires were thin on the ground, unfortunately, but, as if to make up for the omission, the scenery was just spectacular. There was much delightful Gothic architecture and, as we climbed through valleys soaked green with rain, we found picture-book towns of little cottages, contented dairy cows and outdoor plumbing.

We even found Bran Castle, the place Bram Stoker is supposed to have used as inspiration for the Dracula story. It didn't look too scary in the broad light of day and the masses of Romanian tourists made the visit an exercise in queuing and patience. In fact, this and the other Romanian castles we saw over a few days of wandering aimlessly in the mountains convinced us that the

Romanian royals were certainly the poor cousins of the European aristocracy.

We ended our track across Romania at the rust-belt town of Hunedoara in the west of Transylvania. We went there to see Hunyad Castle, a medieval pile started in 1409 with major extensions about 1446, but stayed because there was a good hotel and it seemed like an attractive little town. The weather was threatening and we had had one of those days when we had trouble finding a bed at a reasonable price. After securing the Elephant and stowing our gear, we changed into our walking clothes and headed off to get some exercise and see the place. What we found was an interesting endnote to our Romanian journey.

Under the planned Soviet economy, Hunedoara was turned into the second largest steel centre in Romania, with the steel mills growing to equal the size of the town. The population grew to 86,000 in a well laid out village of ugly Soviet-style apartments, wide streets and lush parks. Like every Romanian town, Hunedoara was clean and neat as a pin. Romanians, it seemed, were neat and tidy people in a way that put the efforts of the Mediterranean countries to shame.

The steel industry was never efficient as raw materials were sourced from India and Canada, but these small details didn't seem to bother central planners. With the collapse of the Soviet Union, however, traditionally protected markets for Hunedoara steel disappeared. The mills were too inefficient and too dirty to compete on world markets and they closed without a whimper leaving half of the population out of work.

More than a decade later things are still tough in Hunedoara, as they are in much of Romania. Jo noticed immediately that there were a large number of second-hand clothing shops along the main street and a visit to the major super market found it well stocked but lacking a big line in luxury goods. Despite these indicators, we were surprised how well the town was surviving. There had been some small reinvestment in the steel industry and several new factories had opened up to take advantage of cheap land and a skilled workforce. The population has dropped by about 10,000, leaving those who remain with a well-appointed and comfortable town. Above all, the town retains the same clean and ship-shape look that we had seen all over Romania.

Dinner in a neat, up-market pizza joint confirmed our view that this was a struggling town. There was clearly no market here for fancy eating. Not even fancy pizza eating! Still, the Romanian beer was good and we enjoyed watching the locals while we munched on two of the most forgettable pizzas we have ever had. In fact, our only real disappointment in Romania was that the regional cuisine was not very strong and most of our meals were lacklustre. The vegetables, in particular, were universally poorly prepared. This was very annoying for two travellers who believe, to deliberately misquote American chef and writer Anthony Bourdain, that you should 'never trust a man who mistreats vegetables'!

Leaving aside the criminal abuse of vegetables, it seemed to us that Hunedoara was symbolic of the whole of Romania. It may have taken a bit of a beating over the last few years, but a strong community pride remained. Whether they had the enterprise to find a prosperous place in modern Europe was open to debate but the place looked to be going in the right direction and the communities were far from dysfunctional. We arrived at the Hungarian frontier on 30 March, thinking positive thoughts about Romanians.

We had set the end of April as our 'get out of Romania' date so that we could be in Budapest for the May Day long weekend. With more than a dozen border crossings under our belt we had found that the best way to cross into a new country was to avoid moving straight from the border to the major city. Instead, we tried to select a medium-sized place that was within one hour's ride from the border. We could then concentrate on getting into town by mid-day with plenty of time to find accommodation and figure out how things are done in the new place. This thinking led us to make our first stop in Hungary the city of Debrecen, located in the east of the country and close to the Romanian border.

Debrecen was Hungary's second city but was a relatively relaxed place. It was also spacious, clean and well ordered, and a great place to get a feel for the country. Our two days there allowed us to come to terms with a new currency, a new (and difficult) language and new customs. We were also able to explore the surrounding area including the nearby Hortobégyi National Park. So, by the time we arrived in the 'big smoke' of Budapest, we thought we had Hungary pegged: orderly, beautiful and Western European expensive! The capital, however, had a few more lessons for us.

Budapest is a truly beautiful city straddling the Danube River. One of those places you just *have* to visit before you die. The trouble with this is that lots of people just *have* to visit it so the place has been inundated with tourists for a long time. There are so many people wandering the streets studying maps that you could be forgiven for thinking there was an orienteering championship underway.

After spending Christmas in Morocco with our daughter Sarah and her husband Mike, we had agreed to meet them again in Budapest for the May Day holiday. As if to confound our planning, however, the Hungarians had organised a four-day weekend for May Day instead of the usual three. As the holiday fell on a Thursday, they took the Friday off as well and made up for it by working the previous Saturday as a normal working day.

The four-day break was well serviced by the cheap package airlines and Budapest seemed to be a prime destination. By the time we got to town, hotel beds for the weekend were thin on the ground and it took a concerted effort over three days to find two rooms in a clean hotel on the Buda (western) side of the river. We were relieved to have somewhere to stay but it was far from an ideal location and much more expensive than we had planned. It seemed that every few days our budget was taking another unplanned hit and that we were spending all of our time taking extreme cost-saving measures to compensate for this.

The rendezvous with Sarah and Mike also had some other benefits. Over the previous weeks we had a number of important items redirected to their London address and they were tasked to bring these on to Budapest. These included a new code generator from my bank to simplify internet banking, as the one I started with had failed; new brake pads for Elephant; and spare parts for our camping stove, which were unavailable in any city we had visited since Spain. The most important items of cargo, however, were our invitations to visit Russia. We had applied for these on the internet at the earliest possible time, 45 days before our planned entry date on 1 June 2008. It had taken the Russians eight days to process the application and a further three days to deliver the invitations to London by courier where they arrived with three days to spare. Without the invitations, there would be no visas.

At the same time as we looked for a hotel we had searched out and visited the Russian Embassy Visa Section. We had reasoned that although our invitation hadn't yet arrived, we could get the other paperwork sorted and identify any other problems. It turned out to be a frustrating visit as we failed to find an official who spoke any English whatsoever. We were simply told, through the good offices of another customer with a little English, that we could only apply in our country of citizenship or residence.

We knew that this was a new Russian policy, but we had hoped that, like the helpful consul in Athens, the Russian Consul in Hungary would agree to hear our special case and agree to process the application. We were given short shrift and the stony, disconnected faces of the bureaucrats left us wondering about the sense of going to Russia at all.

We left before tempers got too heated and our relationship with the Embassy staff suffered irrevocable damage. By then it was Wednesday afternoon and the four-day break was on us so we made our way back to the hotel and settled in, ready to enjoy the weekend with Mike and Sarah.

The support team arrived with the invitations, brake pads and all the other stuff we were waiting on and it was a delight to see them. We spent an indulgent touristy weekend and by the time the two Londoners left in a taxi for the airport, we felt that we had 'done' Budapest. We had also had enough of the bus-loads of other tourists swarming around us.

In our first few days in Hungary we were introduced to Hungary's famous wine Tokaji (Tokay in English), and it was a delightful experience. Although Tokaji wines include dry styles, it is the sweet topaz-coloured Aszú wines that are better known outside Hungary.

These wines were made by adding grapes affected by the benevolent fungus botrytis to the must (the juice and skins of the wine grapes) to produce a sweet, high alcohol content wine. The amount of hand-picked botrytised grapes added to a barrel of must was measured in puttonyos (baskets) with Aszú wines typically having a three to six puttonyo rating on their labels. Generally, the more puttonyos the more expensive the wine and the 5 puttonyo bottle we shared with Mike and Sarah on their last night in Budapest was eye-wateringly dear. It was also superb and a great way to end our few days together in Budapest.

Our arm wrestle over the Russian visas dragged on into another week and consumed our days. The Russians steadfastly refused to give us special consideration and by Wednesday the only realistic plan was to dispatch our passports back to Australia for processing by the Russian Consul in Canberra.

I rang Canberra to confirm that they would process the visa application and to confirm what paperwork they needed. I then rang our son, who works in Canberra, and confirmed that he could receive the passports, process them through the Russian Consul and then dispatch them back to us. We spent hours completing, checking and rechecking the application forms downloaded from the website of the Russian Embassy to make sure there were no mistakes. We could not afford to have the applications rejected on a technicality.

We also had letters prepared confirming our citizenship, we than packed all the documents in a document folder at the DHL office and dispatched them to the DHL Document Centre not far from where our son worked. With this, the first part was done but it was no cause for celebration. We were still not entirely sure that the Russian Consul would give us the visa.

With at least 10 days before our passports returned, we finally escaped from tourist central in Budapest and rode south to find lodgings in the provincial city of Pécs (pronounced 'Paytch'). This beautiful and sleepy university town is 200 kilometres south west of Budapest and was a good base for exploring the wine-growing district of Villány and the Drava Duna National Park. We found a cheap panzio (pension) and settled in for a couple of days.

The city was very pretty, but like the other Hungarian provincial towns we visited, it was very quiet. With time to kill, we visited a number of the small museums in the town including one dedicated to the work of Csontváry, a modern realist painter and contemporary of Picasso.

On the same street we stumbled upon two sections of iron fencing on which people had attached thousands of padlocks. The locks were connected one to another in a mass of brass and steel that was quite arresting when we came across it by accident. We didn't find out how this custom started, but we were told by a local that the locks were put there by couples who use them as a symbol of the strength of their relationship. Many of the locks had been engraved with the names of the couples. Others had the names written in felt pen. Always the cynic, I looked closely to see if any had been severed with bolt cutters to symbolise a failed relationship! Or perhaps the faded felt pen examples were just one night stands.

In Pécs we finally started to come to grips with Hungarian food and drink. Our main conclusion was that a vegetarian would starve to death in Hungary. Meals included huge slabs of meat with little by way of vegetables except the ubiquitous fried potatoes and sauerkraut. Our first night dinner in Pécs, for example, would have sent the average vegan into apoplexy. The ham hock on my plate must have come from the biggest pig in Europe. It was simply huge. I sat staring at it, slack-jawed, with Jo laughing at my surprise. The laughter only lasted as long as the arrival of her pork chops which spread over the edges of her plate leaving only room for a few desultory fried potatoes to squeeze onto the edge.

We set about our meal with intent and it was, to be fair, delicious. But it proved hard work and a hopeless task. The landlord looked at the half eaten remnants with a worried frown and an earnest inquiry. The food was fine, we assured him, but we just didn't have much of an appetite that night after a big lunch. As we found out, a big lunch was no excuse for not eating all your dinner in Hungary!

One night Jo, always one for the vegetarian option, ordered a vegetarian pizza ignoring my raised eyebrow. This was not a cuisine that put a lot of effort into the vegetarian options. The pizza arrived, made with tinned corn and peas and not much else. We ordered a second beer to wash it down. As we had travelled north we had left the salads and olives of the Mediterranean behind and moved into root vegetable country. Never mind; the slow cooked pork hocks were fantastic. You just needed to spread them over two meals and the delicious goulash soup was always a wonderful meal in itself.

We didn't find the great Hungarian red either despite a thorough search, but the discovery of real Hungarian Tokay more than made up for the failure. We also gave Hungarian beer high marks, so much so that we signed up for a tour of the local Pécsi Sörfözde brewery. Our guide, Norá, showed us around this small but modern brewery and was also able to answer some of our more general questions about the city and its people. We finished the tour with a glass of the local product and a pleasant stroll back across the city in the lengthening twilight.

Our meander around southern Hungary led us on to the town

of Siófok on the southern shore of Lake Balaton. The towns around this large lake are the seaside resorts you have in a landlocked country; all the fun of the Gold Coast with none of that pesky surf and no sand in your pants. Unfortunately we arrived on the Sunday of a long weekend and the place was crowded with holiday-makers soaking up the spring sun.

As the previous week had included a four-day weekend for May Day, which had caused us some accommodation problems, you will understand how surprised we were to be caught out two weeks in a row. It took us an hour of shuffling around to find a bed but we ended the week in adequate digs with a bottle of local merlot and a box of treats from a Hungarian cake shop so life was still very good indeed.

Our son Nick did a great job with the Russian Consul in Canberra and had our passports back with the courier within two days of their arrival. He sent us a message to confirm that, with luck, we would have them in Budapest by Tuesday 20 May leaving us a full 10 days to cover the 2000 kilometres north to the Russian border in Estonia to make our planned crossing. Our problems getting the Russian visas meant that we were spending a little longer in Hungary than we had planned and that we would have less time to spend with the Poles, Lithuanians and Latvians and so on. It did, however, give us a great chance to settle into Hungarian life and meet the locals.

Often the kangaroo sticker on the back of the bike was sufficient to start a conversation. In the village of Balatonfüred, a lady named Babi saw the Elephant and whisked us into her kitchen for chilled brandy (at 3pm the sun was over the yard arm). These sorts of events happened often enough that we accepted the invitation without the slightest hesitation and got out our tiny computer to show her some photos to make up for our lack of a common language. We were continually amazed at the ease with which people would buy into our adventure and express real delight at what we were doing. Here, as everywhere, it was the kindness of strangers that often made the day worthwhile. It was also the kindness of strangers that pushed us on.

Just when we were planning our final swoop into Budapest to rescue the passports, Jo received an SMS from an old friend, Jan Cashman, to say that she and her husband Gavan were in Croatia and asking if we could meet in Hungary somewhere. This was too good an opportunity to miss so we adjusted the schedule again and headed back to Budapest and the City Centre Apartments where we had stayed on our previous visits. Our landlady Connie must have wondered if we would seek Hungarian residency after three stays in three weeks!

There was nothing more we wanted to do in Budapest and we opted out of the job of tourist guides for the Cashmans. They were inveterate travellers and didn't need us holding their hands, but the stopover gave us three great nights when we could cook for ourselves, catch up on news from home and swap travel stories. It turned out to be a fortuitous lay-over because the day before we arrived, our little computer went on strike. We think the problem was caused by a virus contracted from a Russian website during our efforts to get a visa invitation but, whatever the reason, we were off the net until further notice.

This was a serious problem. Since our departure we had relied on our computer to keep in touch with our family and friends and also to manage our financial affairs. A broken computer would be a serious setback and the loss of the data it contained could be enough to end our journey there in Hungary.

The computer was also the main (but not only) storage for several thousand photos we had snapped along the way, our primary research tool, the preferred method of pre-booking critical services and the main device for our telephone conversations home. The failure was an 'oh shit!' moment that left a sick feeling in the pit of my stomach and sent me scurrying through the now familiar streets of Budapest following leads to a computer technician. After a half-day search I returned to an internet café we had used a few weeks before where I found a someone who offered to help.

Our new-found best friend spent a full day trying to recover our system without success. Although we could access the drive from another computer, a fix to the operating system was beyond our capability. Whatever virus had damaged the data had done a truly excellent job.

Finally, at 8pm, having exhausted every other option, I decided to reformat the drive. This meant that we would lose all of the programs and all of the data from our hard drive. Although Jo and I had backed up most of our data on USB sticks as we travelled, it was still a significant setback.

Between 8pm and 1.30am the next morning we rebuilt the computer using free-ware from all over the net. Team Elephant was back in business and still had all its critical data. I staggered back to the apartment and flopped into bed. The total cost of the repair was €20.

In the middle of all this untidiness, I had the local BMW dealer service Elephant and walked downtown to pick up our returned passports with their newly added visas for Russia. We had been in Hungary far too long, we had itchy feet and it was past time to go.

On Thursday 22 May we parted company with the Cashmans,

who headed west into Austria, and hustled Elephant north across Slovakia and Poland making good time despite the awful roads and heavy traffic. The spring weather had retreated and we rode on in 10^0 C cold and drizzle but we were now sure we were going to Russia and we were in a hurry. By the evening of 24 May we had travelled 1000 kilometres north and were overnighting in a hotel on the Polish border with Lithuania. Our tails were up, we were both in good health and we were looking for adventure.

10

An Introduction to Russia

After spinning our wheels for a couple of weeks waiting for our Russian visas, we hustled north out of Budapest with a tank full of pent up energy. We took a deep breath and bolted straight across Slovakia and Poland. By the time we reached Vilnius, the capital of Lithuania, we had got the worst of our need for movement under control and we slowed to take our time through the Baltic States of Lithuania, Latvia and Estonia.

These three tiny countries are huddled together at the eastern end of the Baltic Sea and share a great deal of common circumstance and history. Together they have an area of less than 175,000 square kilometres. To put this in perspective, Scotland, with an area 78,782 square kilometres, is larger than any of these countries. The populations are equally diminutive. Estonia can muster only 1.3 million souls, the others just over 2 million each.

We knew very little about these countries and so decided to spend a few days in each, staying in the capitals, Vilnius, Riga and Tallinn. The ride across Lithuania was easy, rolling through the fertile plains of Northern Europe in cool, but not unpleasant, weather. The small villages on the main road seemed poor, but clean and neat and there was plenty of spring activity in the fields. Traffic thickened near the capital and the road widened from one to two and eventually three lanes going our way and dragging us unerringly into the centre.

Vilnius had the feel of a well-ordered provincial city and with 500,000 residents. It was relatively easy to get around and had a lot of churches of almost every type. Apart from Russian Orthodox, there were Calvinist and other Reformist piles together with Roman churches from a dozen different religious orders honouring a spread of saints to meet every taste.

Since the churches were the main feature of the city, we ended up visiting about a dozen of the notable ones but, by mid-afternoon, I was tired and feeling a little distracted. I remembered a group of Irish pilgrims we had seen in the Bascilica in Esztergom, Hungary. They were, apparently, so overcome by the experience that they spontaneously burst into a hymn. I, on the other hand, didn't know any hymns so outside in the carpark I started to hum, and then sing, the only fitting song for which I knew all of the words: Janis Joplin's *Mercedes Benz*. After three verses Jo relented and we went to look for coffee.

Vilnius is built at the confluence of the rivers Neris and Vilnia. The course of the Vilnia has been moved over the years as the city has grown. It now includes a number of islands including one that is the artistic quarter of Užupis, which has cultivated a Bohemian look. Interestingly, the area has declared itself a 'republic of artists'. It has its own constitution, president and anthem, none of which sounded very bohemian to me. Still, it was a shady, quiet place away from the city traffic and for that alone we had to support the artists' pretensions of independence.

Lacking a critical mass of land, population, industry or political influence, all three of the Baltic States have been occupied by one foreign power or another for most of their millennium long histories. Vilnius, pretty town that it is, was also a convenient stopping off place for everyone from German crusaders to Napoleon, who was just passing through on his way to invade Russia. They have all left their mark on the city and its people.

Further on up the road, in the Latvian capital of Riga, we found out how deeply the feelings about Russian occupation ran. The Museum of the Occupation of Latvia was housed in a building as sinister looking as much of its content. There is no doubt that the dead hand of Soviet rule treated these countries badly. There is also no doubt that museums like this will keep the memory, and the resentment, alive for future generations.

Riga had a very beautiful old city that was squeaky-clean, neat and set aside for the tourist. Since we had long since stopped considering ourselves tourists in the sense that its architects recognised, we walked around self-consciously trying to avoid taking a touristic interest but enjoying the place anyway. It was one of those towns where we found ourselves almost subconsciously looking in the window of estate agents for the price of apartments. That is, until we remembered that average winter temperature is about -5° C!

The architecture in Riga is an interesting mix of restored traditional buildings of the plentiful local timber and later concrete buildings. The largest of these was a huge Soviet era monolith reminiscent of the Empire State Building and nicknamed 'Stalin's Birthday Cake' by the locals. The building looked heavy and incongruous and we discovered it had been built in the 1950s to house the bureaucracy looking after collective farms.

We wandered over to have closer look and enquired at the front desk if we could go to the top to see the view. We could. We paid a small fee and were escorted up several elevators and several flights of stairs, through working offices and heavy doors to the observation deck and a grand view of the city and the river delta.

As was often the case, we had the place to ourselves and took our time to study the city detail and take some photographs while our guide waited patiently inside and out of the cool wind. Although the building was totally out of place in this elegant city it did have a great view! It was also worth reminding ourselves that the purpose of the building, the collectivisation of agriculture, was a complete disaster which caused the failure of the agricultural sector. It was, if nothing else, a monument to folly.

Our final stop in the Baltic States was Tallinn, the capital of Estonia. This delightful little city had only 300,000 residents so hardly rated as a 'big smoke'. Rather, it had the feel of a comfortable, provincial town. Its historic centre was beautifully presented and well appreciated by the thousands of tourists that arrive each spring. We found a friendly ramshackle hotel a short walk from the old city, secured Elephant in the yard and stowed our gear in a tiny third floor room. When we came back down to walk the city, we found some of those tourists in the hotel bar.

We discovered over the next two days that Tallinn was a favourite destination for package groups out of the UK that often selected it for stag- or hen-weekends. It would be good to report that they came for the beautiful old city, interesting history and friendly locals, but this wasn't the case. What Tallinn offered was cheap accommodation, very cheap and readily available grog, and cheap sex. It would also be good to report that the cheap and excellent cuisine was on the tourists' agenda but this too had failed to impress. The visitors had spawned a business providing all day English Breakfasts, complete with baked beans and greasy fried eggs. If the group staying at our hotel was typical, they were mostly drunk and mostly obnoxious most of the time. Wonderful!

We felt all of this was a great shame because we really liked the town and found plenty to entertain ourselves with without binge-drinking and abusing the bar staff. One day while walking in the old city we noticed a lot of security and several roadblocks. A motorbike cop told us the Prime Minister of France was visiting. A few minutes later, while we were looking at the Cathedral, the official party and a huge gaggle of extras snaked into the square and around the other side of the building. Not being well adapted to the role of innocent bystander, we headed off to look at other things and to get our hair cut.

The collapse of the Soviet Union in 1991 provided the first real opportunity for independence for the Baltic States and . All of them had been dominated by one external power or another throughout hundreds of years of history. Even together, if they had been able to reach agreement on anything substantive, they lacked the critical mass of land, people, industry or wealth to maintain their independence. It is no surprise, therefore, that by 2004 all three countries had sought the solidarity of NATO and EU membership. It was certainly their best chance of carving out an independent future.

One impact of such a long period of occupation has been the interesting solutions these states have arrived at to decide who is a citizen. The Russians had an active policy of settlement, including the settlement of retired military personnel, which resulted in a good percentage of the population being ethnically different to the nationalists who sought independence. This has led to some somewhat convoluted rules on eligibility for citizenship.

While we were in Riga we noted a letter to the editor of a local paper complaining that the writer had been in Latvia for more than 10 years and was still banned from some clubs in the city that were restricted to Latvians. It was a sudden reality check for both of us. We were simply not used to countries as homogeneous as many of those we had been travelling through. We had both grown up in a diverse city of a genuinely diverse land and we were often surprised at the strength of the xenophobia lurking below the surface in many societies. Of course, none of this had much affect on us as travellers. We were considered remote enough, white enough, Western enough, and sufficiently benign to be welcomed in most places.

Our visit to the Baltic States was relaxing and enjoyable (put these places on your must visit list) but as our Russian visas allowed entry any time after 25 May, and the mid-Spring weather was pleasant, our Russia clock was running. On Saturday 31 May we turned east, spent our last Estonian currency on six litres of 98 octane and two cups of coffee a few kilometres short of the frontier and sidled up to the infamous Russian border bureaucracy.

From the opening round at the vetting gate I knew we were in for a tough day and my confidence sagged. The problem was simple enough. We didn't have the original of our registration papers for Elephant. The registration had expired not long before and we had renewed it over the net. There had not been time to have the original documents sent forward so we had asked Jo's sister Pauline to recover the renewal from our re-directed mail, scan the form and the sticker and email them through to us. I had printed the best quality facsimile of the form possible at a business centre. For the registration label, I took the scan to a fast-photo shop and had it scaled and printed on quality gloss paper. The label was then trimmed to size sealed in a plastic sleeve and fitted to the label holder.

The label was an excellent job, identical to the original, and it remained on the bike until renewal time. The form, on the other hand, was obviously a copy, and copies were not acceptable. Jo remained to secure the bike and I marched determinedly between bureaucrats refusing with offended earnestness to accept that the form was not the correct document. I told them that these transactions were all done over the internet (true) and that the label on the bike was the important document that showed ownership (not quite so true). They refused, I persisted and the hours went by.

I had found a junior guard, a young woman, who spoke a little English and enlisted her to translate my story to her boss. I took him to the bike to show him the label and the details that corresponded between the label and the form. He remained unmoved but I kept insisting that there were no other documents that could be provided. There was no green-card vehicle passport system, as was used in Europe, and these documents were all there was, I insisted. Eventually, and probably through sheer frustration with my persistence, the supervisor relented and told me I could go through.

I found the cashier and purchased Russian insurance for three months to cover the full duration of our visas then returned to the border office where an entry document for Elephant was prepared. The document was in Cyrillic but when it was explained that it was the entry document for the bike I signed it and paid another administrative fee for the privilege. It was a signature we would come to regret a month down the road.

Finally, at four in the afternoon we had our passports stamped and rode out of the frontier checkpoint and into Russia. As we blasted up the goat track that passed for a highway towards St

Petersburg we were both as elated as we had been nine months before when we started our journey. After all, this is what we had come for: Russia, the big Gorilla, 12,000 kilometres across. We couldn't say we had ridden around the world until we had ridden across Russia and now we were ready to try.

St Petersburg is in the top left-hand corner of the Russian Federation and was, therefore, the logical place to start a crossing of this country that would finish at Vladivostok, located in the bottom right-hand corner. It was a bonus that this was a legendary city, famed for its beauty, its cultural treasures, and its heroic history in defying the Nazi Army in a bloody two-year siege.

We knew the city would be easy enough to find (it is hard to miss 4.5 million people), but our pre-booked hotel was another concern. We had no paper maps and only some general digital maps for the GPS. The best we could do was to find the latitude and longitude of the suburb from Google Maps, pick a point and set it as a GPS destination, and then use this as a general guide of direction through the city. As it turned out, this took us through the centre of town on a busy Saturday, but it did get us to the correct suburb where one stop for directions at a service station had us settled with time to spare. It seemed that we were getting good at this sort of thing.

St Petersburg is on the delta of the Neva River and has water, and mosquitoes, everywhere. It also has some attractive canals complete with ferries to move the locals and tourist boats to move the tourists. The canals were flanked by some of the most elegant of the old houses and the view along some of the canal streets was spectacular. I particularly liked the view along a canal to the 'Church of the Saviour on Spilled Blood' with its colourful 'onion' domes shining in the late afternoon sun. Much of the public architecture was monumental, some of it spectacular and some grotesque. Amongst all of this we found few reminders of the destruction of WWII but on one street a stencilled sign on a city wall had been kept fresh as a memorial to the siege. It warned citizens that they were on the side of the street most dangerous in an artillery attack!

Although we stayed way out in the suburbs, where the tariff was still extortionate, getting around was easy. The city had a great metro system. It was fast, clean and cheap, and a long way underground. It dropped us in our suburb, which was a tourist-free zone near a supermarket. The first time we went in to buy some dinner on the way home we were reminded of the time during the Cold War when there were many shortages of consumer items in the USSR. The belief in the West at the time was that it was no use talking to people about human rights if they had other, more basic, problems on their mind, like feeding the family. It was obvious at the first stop that the Russians had achieved The Freedom of the Sausage. We were yet to see if this translated into other freedoms as we had hypothesized with such certainty at the time.

Of course, the thing that everyone *has* to see in St Pete is the Hermitage; the rightly famous museum and custodian of a goodly share of Western Europe's cultural heritage. We duly lined up with the crush for tickets. The building itself is impressively large without being excessive in the way of other grand buildings. We queued for an hour to get in and intentionally left our camera behind so that we could concentrate on the art. This turned out to be a mistake, not because we needed a digitally enhanced a Matisse or two but because the antics of some of the other visitors were worthy of recording.

The Hermitage was simply amazing! There were so many works

by each of the important artists that they fought for space in this gigantic complex. There were rooms full of Picassos, truck loads of Rembrandts, a shed full of Renoirs, Gauguins by the dozen, and a gaggle of El Grecos. It would have taken a week to give the displayed part of the collection a cursory once-over. The millions of pieces not on display were another story altogether.

Jo had done some excellent research on the collection and we concentrated our day on the major European art. We bypassed all galleries that were not on the plan, made straight for the areas of interest and stuck to our task all day.

The place was crowded and it was impossible to ignore the crush. Two groups struck us as interesting. The first were the digital camera users. Having paid a small extra fee to use their cameras, they rushed up to each painting pausing long enough to focus it on the screen, before pressing the shutter and rushing off. We wondered what they might do with the images. Did they take them home, blow them up to life size and study them at their leisure? Would this allow them to understand the emptiness in the eyes of Picasso's Absinthe Drinker? And how did they reconcile that they had only ever seen these things vicariously through a 2 inch LED screen?

The second group of interest was the tour group inmates. They caterpillared their way through the building; milling along. Each group followed a leader holding aloft a marker showing the name of their cruise ship or tour. They walked on in silence as each individual had a headset connected to a small radio receiver. The guides talked continually into a headset-mic pointing out some facts of interest for selected exhibits as they passed. There was time only for a glance. No time to linger. Often these groups would pass in opposite directions. Clusters of ageing Americans and well-to-

ithern Tunisia: salt pans and desert.

ew days of unseasonal snow in Greece...   ...made special treats all the more special.

A picturesque morning tea stop in Greece.

The Western Russian cities were stunning, safe and had excellent metro systems.

Another world-class Russian snarl-up. Traffic that bad takes real skill.

e bike centre in Moscow, looking like a set from *Mad Max 2*. It was run by Russia's est bike club, the Night Wolves.

kers' tea with Ksenia and Andrey. Newly introduced, severe drink-driving laws in ssia meant even bikers here avoided alcohol with lunch.

These knobby tyres were destroyed by less than 2000 km of Siberian roads.

A typical Siberian guesthouse.

Only a handful of riders cross Russia each summer and, with only one road, each team hears about or meets most others. Meetings are warm, with intense information exchange

ur visit to Mongolia coincided with rioting triggered by the recent elections. By the ne the smoke cleared, there were five were dead and 300 injured.

quick oil change between showers in Irkutsk.

The Russians were making a big effort on their trans-national road. When we crossed about 3000 km of it would best be described as 'under construction'.

A balmy summer morning in Siberia.

Team Elephant arrives in Vladivostok with everything intact, including sense of humour (essential equipment for an independent crossing of Russia).

st day in Russia. Elephant and Mike wait on the Zarubino dock while officials argue er the paperwork required to board the Dung Chun Ferry.

Staff of the Korean shipping company give Elephant a good clean in preparation for a rigorous inspection by the Australian Quarantine & Inspection Service.

Day 336, and Elephant's grand adventure comes to an end.

do Japanese, each listening to their own drummer, played out a silent ballet of sidestepping, worried only about falling behind the voice in their heads. Some group tours were no doubt better than others, but it seemed to us that most would simply enable the members to say that they had been to the Hermitage, and maybe to recall a few facts, but nothing more.

Our final observation on the Hermitage concerned the exhibition itself. There were so many exhibits jostling for wall space that much was not shown to advantage. Most of the paintings were framed in glass that reflected the poor lighting, overlaying a reflection of the observer that caused us to constantly shift position to see different details. Some were so poorly lit that a clear view was not possible from any angle. From our uneducated and parochial view, a display with fewer exhibits, better presented, would have been preferable. The excess could be spread around other museums. Despite these churlish observations, however, we were very pleased we went and satisfied that the US$16 entrance fee was well spent.

Having arrived in St Pete through the centre of the city, we had cunningly planned to escape by heading out to join a ring-road running around the eastern boundary. We found the ring-road without trouble and thought we were onto a winner as we thundered south on an eight-lane freeway. Our smugness lasted about 15 kilometres until the traffic ground to walking pace and we found ourselves trapped in the middle of a good old-fashioned traffic jam. The Elephant got hot. Ancient Ladas boiled and stopped in the middle of lanes adding to the congestion. Old trucks which covered everything in a pall of black diesel soot were also prevalent. It took more than an hour to inch forward to the cause of the problem and break free. Six lanes over a new bridge merged into two lanes at the place where an on-ramp added traffic from the city! We were starting to learn that the Russians do things differently.

With the drama of getting to Russia behind us, we decided to break the journey from St Petersburg to Moscow with a stop at the town of '(Velikiy) Novgorod'. This ancient Russian town was an important part of the formation of the Russian nation and culture and it wore its heritage with considerable pride and style. Located on the Volkhov River, we loved the way that the locals had created a little beach culture on a short stretch of sandy shoreline right below the wall of the Kremlin.

Our other interesting find in (Velikiy) Novgorod was the huge Millennium of Russia monument in the centre of the old city. It was unveiled in 1862 and has all the important characters of Russian history in three levels of statues and base relief. We entertained ourselves for an hour wandering around it and trying to identify the players. In 1944 misguided German tourists (the uniformed kind) cut it up and were ready to ship it back home. No wonder people here were suspicious of strangers!

The two-day run down to Moscow was also notable for our first encounters with the notorious Russian constabularies (there were many). The first was a show-and-tell with a radar gun, which resulted in a stern warning, a big grin and best wishes for our visit. The second ran closer to the script. I was invited to sit in the police car where my passport and driver's licence were checked, and then retained. I was told that my traffic offence, whatever it was, was a serious one and there was a fine. I would have to go to the bank and pay the fine then take the bank receipt to the police to clear the offence.

We discussed the difficulty of this procedure for a while until

I asked if he would do me a favour and sort it out for me if I gave him some money. It was not usual he said, but it was possible. I handed over some crumpled Russian notes that I'd kept separate from my wallet and money belt in exchange for the return of my documents, we shook hands, and I got out of the car. As I walked back to Elephant, Jo asked what had happened.

'We just got two tickets to the Policeman's Ball,' I said.

Jo just frowned. We had only just started in this country and already the corruption tax was biting us. The Elephant disapproved of all of this, grumbled a bit, and spent the afternoon being naughty and 'splitting lanes' in the heavy traffic.

I was not too unhappy about the way we had handled our first confrontation with Russia's notorious police. I certainly didn't intend to allow myself to be bullied, and by keeping a small amount of money separate from my wallet and money belt I could maintain that it was all I had and would therefore have to do. Later I would become much more expert and start refusing to pay the amount asked for saying it was too much and that I would pay the fine. As we would find out, the amount of paperwork and administration that paying a fine caused the officers made it a very unattractive proposition for them. They would certainly offer us a big discount in order to avoid their part in the administration of justice.

We arrived in Moscow on a sunny spring afternoon. The traffic was almost a pleasure after the run down, which was saying something as this was a huge city (more than 10 million souls) with world-class traffic congestion! It was also monumental and beautiful, clean, safe and well organised. We only had a few days in Moscow and, in addition to seeing the sights, we had a lot of administration to get done, but all this proved to be less of a task than we had anticipated thanks mainly to the efficiency of the Moscow metro. This masterpiece of organisation moved 9 million Muscovites each day with admirable speed and very little fuss, and, at 75 cents a ride, it was also affordable to all.

We stayed at a hostel that was cheap in Moscow but dear anywhere else in the world. Moscow was a frighteningly expensive city. We rode the subway and walked, and walked, and walked. By the time we had organised our Mongolian visas and done the main sights, we had covered 30 kilometres on foot around inner Moscow. This was another city that we knew pretty well pretty quickly!

Interestingly, the Russians had told us we would have a terrible time with the Mongolians as they were 'so bureaucratic'. On the basis that it takes one to know one, we expected the worst. What we encountered was a friendly and helpful consul who sorted the papers, relieved us of US$90 each, and had us out the door with our visas in record time. Our Russian visas, in comparison, took months to organise and cost about US$750 each. We thought for a moment that there must be another Mongolia, one that was home to hordes of dreadful bureaucrats, but quickly decided that argument was unconvincing.

The Kremlin was spectacular without being ostentatious. Red Square wasn't red at all. In fact, they were setting up a stage for an Independence Day celebration, which seemed decidedly un-Red to me. St Basil's, at the end of the Square, looked better in real life than it had in the glossy travel brochures. Inside, however, we were surprised at how small and pokey it was. The modern city was bustling with cafés and restaurants, throngs of tourists and masses of locals. The place looked and felt like other major Western European cities and was priced accordingly.

The best thing by far about our visit to Moscow was our chance meeting with Ksenia and Andrey, a Moscow biker couple we met through a chance internet contact. Hearing that we were having difficulty finding affordable accommodation, they kindly offered us a billet at their flat. Unfortunately, timing and location combined to stop us taking advantage of their offer. We did, however, catch up with them on a warm Sunday afternoon for a ride around Moscow.

With Andrey setting the pace on a Yamaha FJ 1300 that looked like it had seen more scrapes than hot dinners, and Ksenia bringing up the rear on her pristine GSX 600 Suzuki, we charged around some of the important Moscow sights like a small demented caterpillar.

We had a wonderful day being tourists and bikers all at once. Although our hosts were modern, sophisticated young professionals, we were delighted to find that they were proud of their country and its heritage and that they knew all the foundational stories and told them well.

We visited the memorial complex at Victory Park and had a reminder of the still raw trauma of WWII in this country. The complex includes monuments to all the armies and fleets that fought in the conflict and a public reference database to help families trace the history of those who served.

On Sparrow Hill we had a great view of the city, including the football stadium where two English teams recently played the European Cup final. When I asked if the English fans had been a problem, Andrey just laughed and said that compared with Russian fans they were nothing to worry about and that the police had plenty of practice at dealing with stroppy crowds! I had no trouble believing him.

In an inner-city park we found a jazz band and an exhibition of underwater photography including a shot of a leafy seadragon, a relative of the seahorse. Since I had seen dragons similar to this on diving expeditions, I enjoyed telling Andrey something about my undersea experiences. We rode past the Russian parliament, the famous White House, and visited the site of Moscow's new Multi-Function Centre but the highlight of the day was a visit to the Moscow Bike Center.

This amazing complex was the home of the Night Wolves, Russia's oldest bike club, and functioned as a drop-in place for all bikers. It was inside a stunning gated complex featuring a coffee shop and restaurant, stage area, bike servicing facilities for travellers, a big screen for outdoor movies, and a clubroom (off limits to non-members). It looked like a set from the cult movie *Mad Max 2* and must have looked pretty eerie at night!

We sidled into the bar and it was here that we discovered another important tidbit of Russian trivia. When I ordered beers all round (as any good guest would) there was much sucking in of breath through pinched cheeks. Andrey then pointed out that the new drink-driving rules were so Draconian that any alcohol on the breath and the police would confiscate your bike and your licence for a half a year on the spot! What made it worse was that if you decided that you would like to 'purchase a ticket to the Policeman's Ball', as we did on the way down from St Petersburg, it would cost you more than your bike and licence were worth. 'Bikers' Tea' in half-litre beer mugs it was, then!

Our strange bike drew the attention of the President and Secretary of the Night Wolves. They both struck me as capable, no-nonsense, fit, and in their prime. They were interested in our journey and offered to provide contacts along the way in case we got into a jam. We were quick to accept. It seemed to us that the Night Wolves would be handy blokes to have around in a crisis.

We kept trying to leave but every time we picked up a helmet someone else turned up for a chat. One fellow identified himself as the editor of the local edition of Two magazine, the Russian edition of the British bike journal. He asked us the usual questions, snapped some photos and asked if we minded him using them in the magazine. A few weeks later we received an email with a link to the article he had written on our journey, complete with a photo of Elephant with the two of us grinning like silly old coots.

By the time we got away and were dropped off at our hostel by Andrey and Ksenia, twilight was fading and they still had a long trip home to their apartment on the outskirts of Moscow. With the engines still running and helmets still in place, our thanks for a wonderful day seemed inadequate, but we were just starting to understand the hospitality of Russians.

The Russians we met in Moscow were always interested in our journey so far and our plans to ride across Russia. Many, when they heard we planned to ride to Vladivostok, raised an eyebrow then proceeded to tell us a horror story about the state of the roads. It was, they said, inevitable that our bike would break; we would need at least four spare tyres and we would, of course, be robbed and murdered by gun-toting bandits. Several even asked what weapons we were carrying!

Now, by this time, we had been travelling for more than nine months and had covered more than 45,000 kilometres through all sorts of roads and through all sorts of weather. We are not easily intimidated but this talk was a little unnerving. Some of the bikers we talked to didn't seem to be flighty types and I was at first reluctant to ignore their advice, but then we started to ask the obvious question: what problems did they have when they went across?

This invariably resulted in a short silence followed by the assurance that while they hadn't done the trip themselves, they had a very (very, very) close friend who had, and their advice was good. It slowly became clear that Western European Russians had little idea what conditions were like in the east and we would just have to find our for ourselves.

By Tuesday evening 9 June, we had finished all our preparation for pressing on east. This included the purchase of a new set of knobby tyres for Elephant as there would be no replacements on the way. The knobbies were intended to deal with the mud or dust (depending on the weather) in Mongolia and the Far East.

We had calculated that it would take ten 500-kilometre riding days to get to Irkutsk near Lake Baikal, where we could stop to service the bike and change tyres. We had planned carefully and were confident we would avoid the foolish mistakes that littered the advice of those who had been before us. Within two days we discovered that in Russia everyone has to make their own mistakes.

We bolted out of Moscow on 10 June having calculated that this was the last day that we could leave and still make a comfortable run to the Mongolian border 6000 kilometres away on schedule. We navigated out of the Moscow megalopolis with relative ease and headed east towards the industrial town of Nizhny Novgorod (formerly Gorky) 450 kilometres away. This was to be our first overnight stop.

We were on one of Russia's major commercial highways and traffic was heavy. Road conditions varied from motorway to goat-track. On the good sections of road we made the best of it and ran hard. On the bad sections, we ground out the kilometres using the Elephant's acceleration to blow past other traffic at every chance. We made the 450 kilometres out to Nizhniy Novgorod by 4pm and started looking for a hotel.

And that was when the wheels fell off. We tried five hotels and none would accept us as guests. They all claimed we had visa irregularities. We were sure of our ground and Jo (who by this time was expert at organising accommodation) pointed out that we were complying with the new 2007 regulations. She was told at one hotel that the new rules were fine for Moscow, but in Nizhny Novgorod they were not applying the new rules and we would have to comply with the old ones.

We discovered later that Nizhny Novgorod had been a closed city in Soviet times; a place where they exiled dissidents like the Nobel Prize (1975) winning physicist Andre Sakharov, and made secret parts for submarines. Folks in Nizhny Novgorod still didn't like strangers and we looked pretty strange. After a couple of hours it was clear they didn't want us in their town.

With the daylight starting to fade we took the hint and left in a hurry looking for somewhere to stay. In a small village 25 kilometres away we rocketed past a café that looked like it might have rooms. I had turned Elephant and stopped out the front in a few seconds. Jo was already off the back of the bike and looking for the way in when I noticed that the staff were all sitting around on some outdoor furniture in the garden. There were about eight girls, all dressed for 'work'. A couple came over to talk to Elephant.

Elephant seemed to be making some real progress with Catherine and Olga when Jo returned with a room key and the barman to open a storage shed for Elephant. Elephant grumbled into action and sulked around to be locked up with the rakes and hoes. We unpacked and carried our gear in past the disco room, complete with mirror ball and bar. We had a room in the quiet corner of the accommodation floor and with the madam positioned at the top of the stairs behind her desk and ledger, we were confident of not being disturbed. Although, after 12 hours on the bike, the thought of a back rub did cross my mind.

Whatever the activities of the 'Helping Hands Motel', we had a quiet night and slept soundly. The rent-by-the-hour leopard skin sheets were a real bonus. In the cold light of the next day we assessed our situation and decided that whatever the legal position, we needed to sort out our visa problem before we continued. There was nothing else for it but to return to Moscow. I pointed Elephant back down the highway and, with rain clouds forming, got down to the business.

Six hours later we were back in Moscow, just a little wet, and two hours after that we had the (un)necessary paperwork in our possession. Pizza, beer and a good night's sleep helped us to reconcile the two days and 1000 kilometres we had just burned and, with an early start and the benefit of having done it before, we were out of the city in under 40 minutes. Pleased with progress, we stopped for a breakfast of pancakes and coffee. With full bellies to set us up for a long ride, we rolled Elephant into the river of traffic and let it carry us along. I looked down at the GPS to check our navigation. The message on the screen was simple enough. 'Go east,' it said, and so we did.

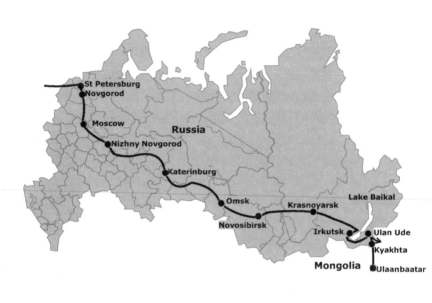

St Petersburg
Novgorod

Moscow

Russia

Nizhny Novgorod

Katerinburg

Omsk   Krasnoyarsk   Lake Baikal

Novosibirsk   Irkutsk   Ulan Ude

                                              Kyakhta

Mongolia   Ulaanbaatar

11

The East

Our return to, and final escape from, Moscow coincided with the first two days of a four-day holiday weekend for Independence Day. We asked every Russian with whom we could communicate from exactly what or whom was independence being celebrated but no one seemed to know. I considered looking it up on the web but in the end thought that if they don't know, I didn't need to. The holiday actually fell on the Thursday but the cunning Russians had all worked a previous Saturday as a normal workday so they could have a long weekend. It seemed to us that we had been the unwitting victims of this scam several times before and we developed a new respect for our hard working and holiday-poor countrymen.

Whatever the reason for the holiday the consequence was an extraordinary amount of traffic on the roads, much of it 'weekend drivers'. As we went back into Moscow it was all going the other way, giving us a dream run. But on Friday the 12th we were in the thick of it all day. Not that a long weekend was needed to make life difficult on the road. The Russians were world class when it came to creating traffic chaos. The roads were a mass of dodging and weaving vehicles, which resulted in many accidents. In a single day we saw 14 accidents on the run from Moscow to Nizhny

Novgorod (450 kilometres). This was more than the total for the 10 preceding months on the road!

Each day was a similar story with a dozen or more accidents in our path. In the built-up areas, each accident created a little more congestion and slowed traffic further. This had a bad effect on the ageing fleet of Ladas and Russian trucks, which expired at inappropriate places creating further chaos. All of this made for a stop-start drive of crazy sprints between jams.

To be fair, some of this was caused by the number of extra vehicles on the road for a holiday weekend but even 4000 kilometres east of Moscow, where the highways are mainly used by long distance trucks, accidents were a daily sight. Statistically, at least, this put the Russians way ahead in the worst-drivers stakes.

We had set ourselves the target of riding 500 kilometres a day for 10 days to get across to Irkutsk near Lake Baikal. We also allowed 5 rest days for sightseeing and to allow us to service the bike and wash off the road grime before crossing into Mongolia within the window we had for our Mongolian visas. With two of our rest days used up in a return to Moscow, we didn't have a lot of fat in the schedule.

Now, 500 kilometres is not a big day in the US, Canada or Australia. Here it was hard work. In addition to the road conditions and drivers, Russians also had to put up with some of the most heavily policed highways in the world. Police check points every few kilometres pulled over vehicles for offences, real or imagined, or just to check documents. We were generally lucky with the police but it was our 10th day on the road in Russia before we rode a full 500 kilometres without being stopped.

On the second day out from Moscow we got mixed up in the vehicles competing in, and supporting the Trans-oriental Rally.

This was a Paris to Dakar type event, although in this case it went from St Petersburg to Peking. We got a chance to chat with some competitors and support staff at a few lunch and overnight stops but lost a lot interest in ever getting involved when we worked out how expensive it was! After a day and a half of riding together, the circus turned south for Kazakhstan and we headed north east into Siberia.

The country itself was quite different from what we expected. The first 1000 kilometres to the Ural Mountains, the area often described as Western European Russia, was green rolling hills much like rural France, but seemingly endless. The Urals, when we did get to them, were a disappointment. They were not much of a range, at their best rising only 2000 metres. Where we crossed, they were no more than some low hills. The romantic moment I had imagined; sitting on the watershed, with the West behind and Siberia and the East in front, passed unnoticed between morning tea and lunch without changing out of top gear.

Beyond the Urals the country dropped down onto the Siberian Plain, which was more than 4000 kilometres across, low and swampy. Here the spring melt-water didn't drain away in the summer, leaving the water table close to the surface or exposed. It made road-building very difficult and most of the main road was raised or 'bunded' above the surrounding plain for vast distances.

The roads varied between four lanes with a good surface (very occasionally) to a badly deteriorated single lane where first and second gear were the best we could do. On the bad roads we did better than any of the cars, often making about 40 kilometres in an hour. Worryingly, the roads continued to deteriorate as we travelled east.

Fuel was relatively cheap (US$1.10/litre) but many stations only sold 80 and 92 octane and this was poor feed for Elephant. The local cars seemed to run fine on 80 or even 76 octane but we had found that this caused Elephant to fart a lot and lose interest in overtaking.

Any area above the water was cultivated and any area with tree cover was wet and therefore not cultivated. The area of arable land was, however, breathtaking. We rode 5000 kilometres through rich black-soil country and only found some higher ground and sandier soils at the eastern edge of Siberia. One consequence of this was that it was difficult to find somewhere to pull off the road for a piss without stepping into a swamp, and our usual roadside lunches were out of the question. Instead of lunch stop picnics, we joined the brotherhood of long distance truck drivers and started to frequent the truck stop cafés and hotels. These places generally had a fuel station (they couldn't be called service stations here as they offered no service), a café and a hotel. We had café lunches of soup, salad, bread and tea for about US$4 each and stayed overnight at the hotels for about US$25 for the room (US$5 extra for a shower) with dinner and breakfast equally good value.

Russian roadhouse food was simple but tasty and nutritious. The café menus were basically all the same with four or five salads, mainly made from root vegetables with a creamy dressing, four or five soups which were mostly ingenious ways of using cabbage, and a few dishes of meat and potatoes. We found an excellent liver soup that was rich with liver, sausage and olives, discovered a few salads that were served without the thick sour cream dressing and these became our favourite lunch fare.

In the evenings, we would have the same salad and soup to start then add a plate of meat and potatoes. We started to eat more cabbage than we could have ever imagined. It was a basic vegetable with most meals and the main ingredient in many soups. There were certainly many interesting ways to prepare it but in the end it was all just cabbage to us.

Obviously, services of all kinds thinned out as we travelled east. This led to one longer than expected day when I failed to take Jo's advice and stop at a suitable pub, claiming we needed to ride an additional half-hour to make it a day. Four hours and 250 kilometres later we were running out of time and options when we finally found an old Soviet-style hotel in a provincial town. We arrived in time to see the town's mid-summer fireworks display but not in time to find anywhere to eat. At least we had made up 200 kilometres on our schedule.

We passed through many very poor rural villages, most of which had no indoor plumbing of any kind. For many villages, wood burning was still the only source of winter heat. The countryside was desperately poor and life seemed tough. This is not to say Siberia was a backwater or even backwards generally. There was a resource and development boom underway and big fortunes were still being made. The cities that were at the heart of the boom were thriving with new middle-class suburbs sprouting like mushrooms and construction cranes filling the sky. We visited supermarkets out there that were as big and well stocked as any in Western Europe. Expensive cars and fashionable clothes were everywhere.

While those cities hooked into the new economy were booming, the agricultural sector had been left behind and those cities and towns built under dodgy Soviet central economic plans were struggling. The hopelessness of growing up in a remote place with only a welfare economy and no prospects for any reasonable future is hard anywhere. In a place where the winters are long and frighteningly cold, we could only imagine the difficulty of life. Satellite TV was available everywhere and the people were well aware that they had been left behind and that no one was coming back to get them.

But despite this, the Siberian locals (and Russians generally) were wonderful people. A request for directions often resulted in a local driving to the destination in his car while we followed or extraordinary efforts to provide maps and instructions we could understand. There was good humour and assistance at every stop. Perhaps it was because of their isolation that the locals were so kind to visitors. In forgotten towns, where no one ever came to visit, the arrival of Team Elephant often gathered a crowd interested in where we had come from, where we were going and, most importantly, why we had stopped in their town. At the heart of this curiosity we felt they seemed reassured by our arrival and the unexpected contact with the wider world.

It became hard to sum up our feelings about Siberia. Antipodeans such as us have grown up in a vast and empty land and have an innate understanding of isolation. The historian Geoffrey Blainey coined the expression 'the tyranny of distance' to neatly describe not only the physical burden of distance, but also its deep psychological impact. But even for us, Siberia was daunting. It flowed out beyond the edges of our comprehension. Each day we pushed further into the endless sameness, chasing our afternoon shadow into the twilight, and each night we reviewed the map to check our progress and felt our hearts sink when we saw how little distance we had covered. We were a long way from home and now we could feel it in our bones.

The end of the road on our transit of the Siberian Plain was the town of Irkutsk, the start of the Russian East and the gateway to Lake Baikal. Of the last 600 kilometres of roads leading to Irkutsk, 400 were very poor and we had stretched ourselves to keep up our average daily distance. Had it not been for our inadvertent 850-kilometre day, when we misjudged the availability of accommodation, we would have fallen short of the ten-day target from Moscow.

By the time we arrived at Irkutsk on 22 June, it was raining steadily and we were keen to get settled in some decent accommodation for a couple of days lay-over. We found some fair digs at a hostel, or should I say they found us, when the owner leapt out of his car and apprehended us as we were about to try our luck at the cheapest pub on our list. We had the place to ourselves on the first night as another couple due to arrive phoned to say that they were in hospital with food poisoning picked up on the Trans-Siberian train, which confirmed our view that rail is a dangerous form of transport. We enjoyed an evening playing house and cooking a simple meal in the kitchen. Meanwhile, it rained steadily through the night.

On the morning of Monday 23 June businesses were open and we set out to find the automotive market to buy some specialised oil to service Elephant. We found the right place without difficulty and were pleasantly surprised to find one of the best automotive markets anywhere. About 200 traders had individual shops gathered inside a single large building. All the shops were modern and very well laid out. It was easy to find what you needed and to compare prices. Once again Siberia surprised us.

All I needed was four litres of fancy oil and, having left Jo standing guard on Elephant in the rain, I didn't want to spend too long inspecting the stalls. I shouldn't have worried. By the time I got back, Elephant had gathered the usual handful of admirers and Jo was having a conversation with a handsome young gentleman about the geology of Siberia (or so she said).

Elephant eventually got a service but only just. Half way through, the rain started to bucket down and, with no shelter, it was hard work to get the basics done. Nevertheless, fresh oil, filter and plugs were a good start and we were pleased that Elephant checked out OK after a tough 12 days.

A treat of our Irkutsk stay was a chance meeting with two German bikers, Emil and Wolfgang, who had come through Kazakhstan and were on their way to Mongolia. They were also BMW-mounted, so it was a great chance to compare notes on Russia and intelligence on Mongolia and to reassure each other that we were all perfectly sane! Emil and Wolfgang were planning to go back to the west from Ulaanbaatar. At the time we discussed it, we all agreed this would be a good route home to Germany but a few days later in Ulan Ude, Jo and I met a Russian biker who had just come over these roads. When we asked him what they were like his one word answer was 'Hell!'. He had fried the clutch on his Transalp Honda and ended his trip to Ulaanbaatar in the back of a truck. He looked pretty used up by the time we met him.

The second treat of our Irkutsk stay was back at the hostel. We were not looking forward to sharing with a group of strangers arriving on the train but we needn't have worried. Chris and Jess turned out to be a delightful young American couple travelling with some of their family and taking a break from teaching in Korea. We didn't meet many native English speakers on our travels, and often went for long periods with only each other for company, so the young Americans were shanghaied to the kitchen where tea was made and stories exchanged.

It was almost comic how much simple pleasure we got from a yarn over a pot of tea with folk fluent in a common language. As is often the case, our recent lifestyle had had the effect of strengthening our appetite for those familiar, almost banal rituals. It was late and still raining heavily when we let the two younger folk escape to bed.

We often felt isolated by our complete inability to understand the Russian language and script but this was seldom a domestic problem. Despite our complete lack of language, we always managed to find a bed and get fed, get repairs done on the bike, and negotiate our way through police checkpoints and border crossings. We each had our areas of responsibility for the administrative tasks we collectively called hunting and gathering. Jo was responsible for negotiating the accommodation while I parked the bike and kept it safe. As she explained it, if she walked into a hotel or guesthouse, she probably wasn't there to buy bread. All that was required was to determine if a room was available, look at the room, signal acceptance, and negotiate the price using numbers written on a scrap of paper. Anything else was a luxury. A similar pantomime was played out in cafés and restaurants. We would often walk around the tables and identify what looked good on other diners' plates then signal to the waiter that this was the dish we wanted. It was a simple system and, if executed with a little good humour, generally got a good laugh from the locals and often an endorsement for our choice from the other diner. In supermarkets Jo always stood back and let me make a fool of myself gesturing and smiling. She had noticed that the women who inevitably served behind the counter were apt to find the foolishness of a bloke amusing, if not charming, but were not so well disposed towards charades by a female.

So, the lack of language didn't stop us travelling comfortably. What it did, however, was limit our understanding of the wider culture because, inevitably, language and culture are intertwined. We could observe and record, but we could never understand without language. It also added to our sense of isolation, which meant any chance to chat with English speakers was embraced. That one night in Irkutsk, at least, we were able to scratch our communication itch.

It continued to bucket down and, as Irkutsk had already established itself as one of our least favourite places to stay in the rain, we decided to head out to Lake Baikal regardless of the weather. A planned early departure turned into a late departure as we had fussed about with our wet weather gear hoping for a break in the clouds (none came). Our discomfort was made worse when we took a wrong turn and exited the city in the wrong direction, forcing us to circle the town and ride back through the centre to get onto the right road. This, combined with torrential rain, heavy traffic and a twisting, poor quality road added up to a 3-hour ride for the 100 kilometres to the first lakeside town. It had only one ancient, run-down hotel but we were not in a choosy mood. We booked in and, while we still had our rubber suits on, decided to walk to a place where Jo had seen a small café.

We trudged off into the rain, slopping through the water. A kilometre went by, and then another, before we found the café, which was, of course, closed. The rain continued to thunder down. We walked to a small shop and bought what food we could, along with a couple of half-litre bottles of beer, then dragged ourselves back through the rain. Our room had never been luxurious and years without maintenance had not been kind. We spread out our gear to dry, organised a hot shower and some warm dry clothes, then retired to bed to keep out of the cold.

The next day we rode on into steady rain as there didn't seem much point in being lakeside tourists in such poor weather. This was a shame because Lake Baikal is worth visiting. The lake is not only huge, it is also deep. Deep enough to contain about 20 percent of the world's surface fresh water, or more water than all five of the North American Great Lakes combined!

But, as the rain continued, our plans for a few lazy days seemed as elusive as the sun and we splashed up the east coast of the lake heading for Ulan Ude. The rain had left the worst sections of the road very muddy, slippery and slow but as the day dragged on the rain lessened, and then stopped, and we arrived in Ulan Ude in a blast of sunshine and humidity. We found an affordable room in the old Soviet era hotel (unrestored to the extent that the original single-station radio was still on the wall) and settled in for three nights.

Top of the to-do list for Ulan Ude was to fit the Metzler knobby tyres we had brought from Moscow and to find a small engineering shop to do a welding repair. The knobby tyres were intended to provide better grip on the poor roads and I was very keen to fit them. The roads had deteriorated consistently as we had travelled east and, with the constant rain, were often very slippery and treacherous. When we changed to the Metzler knobbies we discarded our well used Michelin Anakees and did away with the additional 15kg we were carrying on the back of the bike. This was very important to me as weight so far behind the back axel has a bad effect on handling and puts great strain on the aluminium frame that holds the back of the bike together.

The Metzlers had been recommended by the service manager at the BMW dealer in Moscow. He assured me that these were the best tyres for the local conditions and ideal for the Far East and Mongolia. By the time we had reached Ulan Ude we had, however, realised that he had probably never been to the Far East and was just elaborating on the urban legends of the West. Like almost everything else we were told about the East by Westerners, this was just nonsense. The Metzlers were nearly a disaster.

We also gave Elephant a bath using a public standpipe near our hotel. Even in larger cities in Siberia and the Russian Far East, many houses were not connected to mains water and people still drew water from public standpipes. This was often done using large milk churns on trolleys and each house had three or four of these to provide water for washing, cooking and so on.

Smaller villages without standpipes drew their water from wells, however, these were often located just metres from the long-drop toilet and this didn't seem like a good idea to us. Our inability to sort out what was probably good water and what was possibly not, caused us to switch to bottled water for our time in Russia. Fortunately, it was readily available and reasonably cheap everywhere we travelled.

Somewhere on our journey I had lost the spark plug spanner from my tool kit. As always with these losses, I subjected myself to all manner of recriminations and made the usual pledges to always double-check everything. Things lost on the road were often difficult or impossible to replace. In true BMW style, the plug spanner was a special tool that could not be replaced by any of the standard plug spanners available in the tool shops we found. My best solution was to buy a cheap plug spanner that was sufficiently thin walled to get into the BMW head and then weld an extension onto it so that it protruded far enough to use. A cheap 10 mm socket was fine for an extension so I took Elephant wandering through the industrial part of town looking for a place to do the welding. We wound around back alleys and muddy lanes for hours past all manner of tiny businesses and workshops until we found a small jobbing shop in which I spied a lathe and a mill. The boss of the place took me to the lunch room, cleared the lunch litter from the only table and studied the small engineering drawing I had done and the two parts I had brought. With the common language of a drawing and some measurements, he knew exactly what I wanted and set to work doing an excellent job with some antiquated tools.

While we waited for the metal to normalise, he and his two workers came out to look at Elephant and study the maps of our journey with a sort of awe that left me in no doubt that here, in the heart of Mongolian Russia, we were so exotic that we might have been from another planet and the fact that we had arrived on a motorbike was just incredible.

After a polite amount of time trying to answer their questions and understand each other, I asked the boss how much I owed for the work.

'Nyet,' he said. 'Welcome to Siberia!'

I knew enough not to argue with this so I smiled and nodded my acceptance. I rummaged in my pocket and out came a crumpled five Euro note which I pressed into his hand and, summoning what Russian I could, asked him to buy a beer for his workers with my compliments. There were smiles and hand shakes all round, best wishes for the journey and a cheery 'da svidaniya' before I sped off to another place and they trudged back to their lathes.

We did a good deal of walking over these few days looking over the town and finding someone to give us our first haircuts since arriving in Russia. Ulan Ude was the centre of Mongolian

Russia and the look of the people and feel of the place was very different from the Siberian towns we had visited until then.

As we had discovered, there was considerable ethnic diversity in Russia but travel restrictions during the long Soviet repression had worked against any broad integration of the groups. It was only since President Putin had assured all Russians they were a free people, allowed to travel wherever they liked, that the ethnic groups were starting to disperse a little. For the most part, however, each culture remained highly concentrated within its traditional boundaries.

Ulan Ude had the vestiges of a faded 19th Century glory, including a huge opera house and some elegant public buildings. It was a scrubby, rough and ready sort of place but a good stop to enjoy some sunny days and catch our breath. The people of Ulan Ude were predominately sturdy Mongolian stock; wiry, athletic and cheerful. The city had been prosperous during the 19th Century, when it was a transport hub for the tea caravans from China. The railway had killed that business and the city had never fully recovered its glory days.

On 28 June we rode down to the Mongolian border and the frontier town of Kyakhta. This garrison town (there appeared to be an Infantry division straddling the road on the way in) also had its heyday before the advent of the railway, when it too prospered from the tea caravans. Today it is another of those dusty border towns full of the characters and desperadoes who seem to gravitate to these places all over the world. The ruins of the city's once spectacular Trinity Cathedral, built in 1817 on the wealth of the China tea caravans, was the story of Kyakhta writ large.

We prepared our papers to cross into Mongolia the next morning. We were less well prepared for Mongolia than for any other place we had visited and the Russians had done a good job of frightening us with stories about the roads and broken bikes. As always, however, we were keen to work it out for ourselves.

Closing up on the Mongolian frontier the day before we crossed allowed us to be second in line when the gates opened. We were feeling confident that we would be through and on our way to Ulaanbaatar in an hour at the most. Five hours later, with both of us feeling dehydrated in the summer heat, the last gate was opened and a bored guard wished us welcome to Mongolia. If our two-and-a-half-hour effort to get into Russia was a black comedy, our exit had all of the style of a Greek tragedy with a chorus of Russian border clerks.

The 'problem' was that the entry document for Elephant was only issued for a period of two weeks and we been in the country for a month. Since it was written in Russian we had no way of knowing it was different from our three-month visas and three-month bike insurance! My failure to pick up this clerical error and my signature on the document was, of course, a heinous crime for which I would have to pay. The interrogation went on for hours and it was pretty obvious the Russian border guards were as unhappy to be there as we were. I had worked in public relations in the past and had plenty of experience of being cross-examined by the most aggressive journalists in the business so I was not backing down from the Sunday shift at a remote Russian border station.

Only one of the guards, a relatively junior young woman, spoke basic English so it was hard work communicating my position but I kept dragging the conversation back to my main claim: the Russian border official had been incompetent on entry issuing a 14 day bike-visa when we had paid for three month's insurance and had three month personal visas. The fact he had done so when he knew I didn't speak or read Russian could at best be interpreted as incompetent and, at worst, an intentional scam. Why, I argued, should I be in trouble for the incompetence of another?

In the end, we got down to the choices. The Sunday shift didn't have the authority to grant a dispensation. I could go back into Russia and stay locally overnight then come up the next day and speak to the Station Chief who had the authority to waive the offence should he choose to do so. Alternatively, I could sign a statement admitting I was wrong, but putting down the mitigating circumstances, pay a fine and then go through to Mongolia that day.

The thought of spending another day in the dusty town of Kyakhta was extremely unappealing. There was nothing else for it but to buy a table for 10 at the Policeman's Ball. I stomped off in the company of my interpreter to the cashier while the clerks typed up a half-dozen forms, each with five copies. When I returned with the receipt, I was asked to sign the statements so that I could go into Mongolia. I refused.

'What now?' they groaned.

'Well,' I pointed out. 'I got into this jam because I signed a document in Russian I couldn't read and you now want me to sign these. I don't see why I should unless I know what they say.'

There was no arguing with the logic, so the poor interpreter sat down and went through the documents with me and explained each one. More hours went by. I added a hand written statement to each in English stating that I couldn't read the document, followed by what I had been told it contained, and signed each one. During the middle of all this, Jo was finally brought in out of the sun and given a place to wait in a little comfort.

I didn't develop any animosity towards these border police as a result of this (or towards any border police elsewhere after other problems we had). I came to see them as just another bunch of poor bastards, stuck in a remote and unpleasant place (even by Russian Far East standards) and saddled with administering a system that was pedantic, and extraordinarily bureaucratic. They remained polite and respectful even in the face of my (equally polite) obstinacy. Before I left I took the time to shake each officer's hand and thank the young interpreter for her perseverance. She gave the embarrassed reaction of someone who hadn't had too much thanks or praise in her working life.

We still had another hour getting into Mongolia but this was a relatively easy if confusing business that seemed to involve acquiring sufficient stamps to completely cover our entry card. On our first attempt, there was some white paper showing and we were sent back to get more. Eventually there was no more room to stamp the form and we were allowed to pass. Once we were through the last gate we fired up the Elephant, charged past the border-town money changers and shysters, and tore into the countryside soaking up the blast of cooling air.

An easy run down to the capital Ulaanbaatar gave us a chance to cool down as we climbed up to 1500 metres. If this was summer, then Mongolia would be bitter in winter. It was, however, pleasant riding and, despite some determinedly silly drivers, Ulaanbaatar was simple to navigate. We had done no preparation for our visit to Mongolia but had no trouble changing some money, finding a good, reasonably priced hotel, and getting ourselves well fed. Fortunately there was no cabbage soup on the menu!

Mongolia was a large country (about the size of Iran or Libya) but with only two million people. More than one million of these lived in Ulaanbaatar leaving the remainder of the country short of urban centres. The city was a dusty (or muddy) crush of humanity full of energy and a little shambolic. Definitely our type of town!

We got our walking shoes on and got some exercise stomping all over the city exploring the back streets and temples and finding interesting little restaurants and shops. Jo bought a silver bracelet with elephants on it as a symbol of solidarity with our Elephant and we found excellent Mongolian cashmere and camel-hair scarves and shawls for the offspring. These were the first tourist things we had bought on our journey and it was sign of our confidence that we were prepared to carry them forward from here.

Walking back to our hotel after dinner one evening we noticed a sign for the Mongolian Harley Club Bar and Grill. We spotted a couple of bikes and went to investigate. We found one guy who spoke some English and another who spoke German, and explained why we were in Ulaanbaatar. Within a minute we were inside the bar drinking beer with a bunch of Mongolian bikers and swapping our stories. One fellow turned out to be a superintendent of traffic police who gave us his card and personal mobile number as a get-out-of-gaol card. As he explained it, if any traffic officer was foolish enough to pull us over, we should simply phone him and hand the phone to the officer. He would do the rest. He told us he had spent three years studying in East Germany; an experience he hated. He had been beaten by neo-Nazi skinheads and had been on the receiving end of some pretty bad discrimination. Another biker ran emergency coordination at the airport, played guitar and sang sad Mongolian songs. Enough beers were drunk to make us all new best friends before we slipped away into the night and made for our hotel.

The following day we took the bike out to ride around the sights and ran into Emil and Wolfgang, the two German BMW riders we had met in Irkutsk. They were on their way to the Russian Embassy to try to sort some visa problem. Later we walked past the Russian compound and found a group of Polish guys on a range of bikes who were trying to sort out their Russian visa problems. A pattern was starting to emerge! They were all on Honda Transalps and they had gear hanging off the machines everywhere. Elephant may have looked ungainly, but compared with this lot, we were neat and tidy on the road.

Our hotel, selected at random, turned out to be the transit place for groups of Australian tourists who were taking the Beijing to St Petersburg train. They were all about our age and had a three-day stop-over in Ulaanbaatar during which they did the required overnight stay in a *ger* (Mongolian *yurt*). While Jo was checking in and I was making sure Elephant didn't wander off, they poured out of the hotel to be sheep-dogged off to lunch by a young guide. A couple of the men came over to look at Elephant and when they discovered that Elephant was Queensland registered, they struck up an animated conversation that drew the remainder of the group.

Jo emerged from the hotel and joined the crush. We were hot in our riding suits but the questions were coming thick and fast. Much to the chagrin of the young guide, they were keen for Team Elephant's advice on Irkutsk, Moscow, St Petersburg and Russia generally. I am not sure the guide appreciated our advice as we didn't think highly of moving around in a large group and didn't think there was any real need for a guide in any of those places. We wished each other luck before they were hurried away but we were sure they would need it more than us. By this time, Team Elephant had its collective tail up. We were full of confidence and full of fight.

On the afternoon of 1 July, we were walking back from the central market when we saw a large demonstration underway in the downtown area. The Opposition had claimed recent elections were rigged in favour of the government and this brought the demonstrators out onto the street. There were the usual speakers revving up the crowd of many thousands. There were no police at the scene, and we didn't see any nearby, but it was all peaceful enough at that stage.

Having always taken the view that there is nothing as pathetic as an innocent bystander, we passed by on the other side of the road and didn't stop to investigate. An hour later and two blocks away, while we were having dinner, the demonstration turned ugly and then degenerated into a riot. The authorities were either caught flat-footed or happy to let it get out of hand, and by the time police reinforcements were on the scene the headquarters of the ruling party was on fire along with the Modern Art Gallery. We watched the riot on the television as we ate; the smell of smoke wafting through the window from the fires just a few hundred metres away.

After dinner we walked in the general direction of the riots to find a shop to buy water. Groups of locals gathered in all the stores and outside on the footpath, transfixed by television screens, watching the unfolding drama while just a short distance down the street everyone could see the red glow of the fire and hear the shots of the just-arrived riot police. When I saw images of the police starting to fire pump-guns into the crowd I knew it was time to be off the streets so we gathered up our water and walked back to the safety of our hotel.

In the end, five people were killed and about 300 injured. By the next morning the government had declared a four-day state of emergency including a 10pm curfew and had put troops on the streets. It seemed to us it was all a day late and a dollar short, and to make matters worse, a ban on the sale of alcohol was included for good measure. We kept ourselves safe and out of harm's way throughout all of this, but one bright spot was a phone call we received from the Consulate in Beijing. They just rang to check we were OK. We thought it was a good service and well worth the effort of filling in the online registration form to let them know our rough itinerary.

We were not sure what the locals made of these dramatic events but there did not seem to be much discussion and reflection. Considering five people died, we were surprised when the events were off the TV and out of the papers after 24 hours. Clearly there was much we didn't understand about this country.

While all this was happening, we got some reasonable intelligence on the road conditions for bikes in the areas in which we were interested and confirmed that the route we planned was possible two up on our heavy bike. What we couldn't confirm was whether the Russians would let us back in through the remote border post we were considering. This posed a significant problem as we would not have the time to retrace our route if we were unable to get through. After the bad experiences we had had at every turn with Russian bureaucracy, we reasoned it might be better to re-enter Russia through the main crossing. This would short-change our Mongolian side-trip, but getting Elephant stuck in Mongolia didn't seem like a good idea either. Almost on cue the skies opened and we had two days of torrential rain turning the city to mud.

We may have been willing to take our chances with the Russian Border Police but it was the state of emergency that finally did for Mongolia. As a part of the package, all border crossings to Russia and China, except one in the north and one in the south, were closed to foreigners. The only way out was back the way we came. Besides, four days without a cold beer just seemed out of the question. Elephant was packed and pointed back up the road towards Russia. By mid-afternoon we had crossed the frontier without drama and were enjoying a late lunch of cabbage soup.

Russian Far East

Skovorodino

Lake Baikal

Khabarovsk

China

Irkutsk

Chita

Vladivostok

Zarubino

Kyakhta

Ulaanbaatar

12

Getting Home

Back in Russia on 4 July, we retraced our steps to the regional city of Ulan Ude to overnight before continuing east. After our fraught exit from Mongolia, we thought a border crossing and a 600-kilometre ride was a good day's work and enjoyed a couple of icy cold Russian beers to celebrate. We felt like old hands navigating into the city centre and chuckled at how quickly we could come to terms with a new city. One day on the bike and one day on foot, we agreed, was all it took to unlock the basic scheme of a city.

The next day we continued east to the city of Chita. On the road we met Polish couple Kamil and Izabela riding a Honda Africa Twin. The Honda weighed about 50kg less than Elephant, but theirs was heavily laden and would have been no easy ride on the gravel. Our store of up to date information on the road ahead grew, along with our confidence. A few hours later we met Yasuhito Konishi, solo on an Africa Twin, who had ridden the road three years previously.

'The road is much harder now,' he said. 'The gravel is awful.'

Our confidence flagged a little.

This was to be our last day of relatively easy riding for some time. We arrived in Chita late and had trouble finding the centre and finding a cheap hotel. The old Soviet-style hotel we eventually stumbled on was run down and shambolic but was a lucky choice in another way. Another rider, Charlie Honner was also staying at the place. He was on his way from Japan to London to take up a new job and thought he would take the scenic route.

A few hours with Charlie gave us further good information about road conditions ahead and hopefully we were able to fill in some gaps for him. By the time we parted Team Elephant was confident it had the most up to date information available on the conditions ahead.

On the morning of 7 July we double checked the load, solved the riddle of the maze which was our way out of Chita, and found ourselves on the road east. We blasted over the first 100 kilometres of tarmac then settled down to the rough ride. The leg from Chita to Khabarovsk was a distance of about 2300 kilometres: not much in this vast land. Of this, a few hundred kilometres were a bituminous surface varying from good to pot-hole alley. The remainder, about 1800 kilometres, was unsealed. To be more technically correct, the remainder was under construction. To put that in perspective, this was a construction site stretching twice the length of Great Britain. In the land of giants, even the construction sites were epic.

A few dozen riders undertake the 10,000-kilometre trans-Russia crossing each summer and, with a single ribbon of road crossing most of this vast land, it was inevitable that each rider would meet or hear about most of the others on the road at the same time. The meetings were often short and intense; each rider, or team, keen to confirm that there were others who would want to do it and desperate for helpful contacts and information about the road, fuel, accommodation, and places to avoid.

Most solo riders make it from Chita to Khabarovsk in about five days. We had intended to take six, out of deference to our seniority and common sense, but ended up taking five. The story of why is really the story of our crossing. Routes M55 and M58, which cross Siberia all the way to the Russian East, had been poorly built and then poorly maintained over many years. The reason for this was easy to see on the ground. The road system was almost irrelevant to the economy and the lives of the people in remote Russia. It was the Trans-Siberian Railway that provided the all-purpose communications network to bind this impossibly big country together. The railway moved the great mass of every kind of resource or supply, around the clock, with impressive efficiency. Development had followed the tracks with a string of towns clustered along the line and sparse development elsewhere. The road had been strangely detached from all of this. Most roads in the Far East were local, intended to distribute goods shipped forward by rail.

There was little incentive to develop a national network and the route was impassable in numerous places from time to time. In 2004, work started on development of a national trans-Siberian road. The re-surveyed route took it further away from the railway and from the railway towns in many places. At the time we crossed it, the surface varied greatly but most was gravel. Gravel! Deep gravel, unconsolidated road-base gravel, riding-on-marbles gravel; every bike rider's nightmare.

For the first two days our ride went to plan. We made the towns we were targeting comfortably and, eventually, found a bed. These towns were desperately poor. Forgotten in the vastness of the Eastern Plains, they were ground down by poverty, dusty and frayed. The log-cabin houses had no indoor plumbing at all and were heated by wood fires. No foreigners came here. No tourists got off the train. Nothing changed.

A typical guesthouse in a lost town called Chernishevsk took us an hour to find with lots of impossible directions from locals. The accommodation consisted of a small concrete-block hut of a single room divided into three areas by partial walls. The central area had a stove, no doubt placed there to better distribute the heat. There were six beds in the house, two in each of the areas. Five were occupied the night we stayed. The house had no indoor plumbing. There was a long-drop toilet at the back of the yard along with a *banya* or sauna room heated by a wood fire. The *banya* was most welcome after a hot and dusty day.

As we travelled east, we shared our accommodation with ordinary Russians; company reps visiting the small shops, delivery truck drivers, electrical engineers working for the power company. We ate in their cafés, discussed the road and the weather and answered, as well as we could, their ever-curious questions about where we had come from and why we were there. The Russians we met started to have faces and names, jobs and families.

On a dusty section of road we saw a couple of big bikes approaching and pulled Elephant over for a meeting. As they emerged from the dust we saw they were all Harley Davidsons, all low-slung cruiser-style bikes. There were 17 in all from the Korean chapter of the Harley Owners Group! They had a support vehicle for all their gear with a trailer behind which had a broken bike on it. The HOGs were on their way to Germany on a grand adventure. They were dressed in a variety of jeans and cruiser boots and jackets. Many had open face helmets with scarves and goggles to keep out the dust.

They had experienced some bike problems along the way and

three bikes had already been damaged, one to the extent that their mechanic couldn't get it running and had retired it to the trailer. As the bikes came in and stopped, the riders clustered around our heavily laden rig looking at the details of the luggage fit, the special knobby tyres, the long travel suspension and lots of other stuff. They were amazed that we had two people and all of our gear on the one bike and that the bike seemed to be handling it well. They even looked enviously at our filthy but serviceable riding suits. Elephant looked down that funny nose at the low-slung cruisers and I must admit that I saw a certain rugged purposefulness in the beast that had eluded me on the freeways of Western Europe. Out here, Team Elephant looked the goods and the Elephant stood tall. Their faces dropped when I told them that they had about 1000 kilometres of awful road before they got to the plain bad road. We could see that they were travelling hard. After the usual good wishes, we stood and watched them ride off into the dust heading west. Later, in Vladivostok, we would hear the Harleys had suffered badly on the way to Chita and all of the bikes had needed repair before continuing. There was no doubt in our mind that the group had been greatly under-prepared and was suffering because of it. When we eventually got to Korea and saw the excellent roads, congested traffic conditions and short distances, we could see how challenging the ride would have been for the Harley riders. Our background at least gave us an intuitive feel for distance, bad roads and isolation.

On the third day it rained, and rained, and rained. We met Masayuki Goto on his Africa Twin again. He was going west, looking cold and tired, but showing the same sense of independence and determination we had seen in all the riders. We reassured him that the road ahead was awful and he did the same for us. It seemed the least we could do for each other.

The road turned to mud. Elephant slipped and slid and we were reduced to a 2nd gear idle. It took three exhausting hours to cover 40 kilometres. There was nowhere to stop so we pressed on throughout the day and into the early evening. We found fuel in the early twilight and learned that there was a hotel in the town of Skovorodino not far up ahead. With options short, we set out to find it.

Thirty kilometres further along the road, we found the sign for the turn-off to Skovorodino. It was one of those large white-on-blue freeway signs and said turn in 300 metres. We turned. The road went 25 metres and stopped dead. We got off the bike and looked around. Beyond a mound of earth blocking the road the land dropped off into a swamp. We remounted, backtracked, went further down the highway, turned around, and found another sign coming from the other direction. Turn in 200 metres it said, but the familiar sideroad remained a 25-metre dead end. This was Russian humour at its best and even after 12 hours on the bike in the rain we got the joke.

We continued east for another 16 kilometres, wondering where we could find a bed, before seeing a small track heading off in the direction in which we thought the town would lie. It had no signpost but we followed it anyway. After a kilometre it was no more than wheel ruts and we started to wonder if we had wasted our time. After a further kilometre we saw a large bulldozer parked in the woods near the track with the operator asleep in the cab. I stopped and Jo climbed off the bike and up onto the track of the giant machine. God knows what the operator thought after being woken from his doze by a stranger in a space suit, but he waved us onwards when asked if this was the way to Skovorodino.

We squelched on through the mud. After about 10 kilometres we emerged from the woods along a creek line and were astounded to see the outline of large buildings through the grey rain. We rode on, incredulous as the outline of more and more buildings formed, until a town of 30,000 souls had emerged miraculously from the mist! The joke, it seemed, was on the Russians: Team Elephant had found Skovorodino.

We also found the hotel, a clutch of friendly, helpful locals who manhandled Elephant up the hotel steps and into the foyer, and a Chinese restaurant that didn't serve rice but did serve chips. It never ceased to amaze us how life could change so quickly on the road. We arrived wet and cold and tired but, with a hot shower, hot food and cold beer, and a little lively interaction with the locals, morale was restored. I should say we felt 'buoyant' but after a day paddling through the wet, that didn't seem quite the right word.

The road dried out on the fourth day and we made better time, sometimes going as fast as 40 or even 60 kilometres an hour! The day was hot and long, food and fuel were hard to find and there was no sign of accommodation in the place we had hoped to find it.

We pressed on. The second planned accommodation option failed to materialise and, with the last of the afternoon shadows fading and only the twilight left to ride, we had 170 kilometres of bad road to the last option. We had received some reasonable intelligence on a guesthouse from our Japanese friend Masayuki Goto so we were confident that we would find the elusive accommodation if we just kept at it.

We pressed on with some determination over some of the worst roads we had ridden and made the distance just on last light only to be told by the locals that there was no hotel or guesthouse for a long way in any direction. Our information on accommodation had clearly been wrong three times out of three!

The roads in this section were constructed of a sand base with loose river gravel up to 10cm deep and were very hard to ride. If Elephant wasn't skating on the stones, the front wheel was burying itself in the exposed sand. After a full day of riding in these conditions I was exhausted, dehydrated and worried that I would fall in the dark. I told Jo we needed to stop.

Our usual procedure was to secure accommodation first, then get food. This night, however, we were not sure there was any accommodation to be found so we decided to fill our bellies and rehydrate while we had the chance. We had dinner at a roadside café where we were asked if we knew another rider named Charlie (Charlie Honner by our reckoning) who could drink vodka like a Russian. Under other circumstances we would have turned this opening into a party, but we were well beyond caring about Charlie's vodka drinking credentials so we lied that we didn't know him then headed Elephant east again on a stretch of sealed road.

After about an hour in the saddle we found a small sideroad, then a track and finally a concealed meadow. It was midnight and we had by then ridden for 16 hours since morning. We organised an improvised shelter and settled down to get a few hours sleep in our 'stealth camp'. Although we did not intend to camp during this journey, on the grounds that we were at an age where we could be excused camping duties, we had a little equipment on hand for such a contingency. In a tube under the back of the bike, there was a tent flysheet and we were carrying a mosquito net in our back box. The mosquito net was more easily accessible because we often used it in hotels that were not screened against the hordes of Siberian mosquitoes which are, unfortunately, prone to carry

Japanese encephalitis. It took only a few minutes to put up the shelter and drag our gear and ourselves inside and only a moment for us both to drop into an exhausted sleep.

In the morning we had a dingo's breakfast (a piss and a good look around) and started early on the fifth day. The road got better, then worse, then better again. We found a roadhouse and blinis and met Edgar from the Russian Black Bears motorbike Club. By then we had only a few kilometres of unsealed road remaining and he had the whole ride to Moscow ahead of him. We wished him luck with some sincerity. Then finally, late on the afternoon of 11 July, we ambled into Khabarovsk and booked into a hotel with plenty of hot water and a double bed.

Throughout our 12,000-kilometre ride across this stunning land we had rubbed along with the ordinary Russians going about their lives. In the remote areas the only foreigners we met were other adventure riders. The locals were friendly, amazingly helpful, curious, cheerful and pleased that we had made the effort to come to their town. We had often said that we were 'propelled on our way by the kindness of strangers', but nowhere was this more so than in the Russian Far East. Although there was always the risk that Elephant would miss-step and put us onto the road, we were confident that the Russians would stop and offer genuine assistance. It was just that kind of place.

Long-distance truck drivers had a particularly tough life. The extraordinary distances, appalling roads, extreme climate and almost complete lack of infrastructure made every trip an adventure. They formed a sort of tough-guys brotherhood, proud of the difficulties they faced each day. We had many conversations along the way with them speaking Russian and us speaking English. They gave us advice about the road ahead, the weather, where to get a bed and the cafés where the cabbage soup was as good as their grandmothers' (at least that's what I think they said). In return we told them the story of our journey, and how pleased we were that we had come to this place.

Whenever they saw bikes, with their grim-faced riders skating around on the gravel, they acknowledged them with a series of horn blasts and a friendly wave. Some punched the air with a clenched fist in the universal salute of the undefeated; the exclamation mark of defiance. We always acknowledged them with a wave and, I have to admit, occasionally a raised clenched fist. After all, we were all tough-guys out there.

The last leg of our 12,000-kilometre journey across Russia was a mere 780 kilometres of reasonable road between Khabarovsk and Vladivostok. Under other circumstances we would have made the distance a day's run but Elephant's rear tyre had been almost destroyed in the 2300 kilometres from Chita to Khabarovsk. Fissures had opened up in the casing and too much more abuse would see it fail. We decided to take a slow, two-day trip down and to look for new tyres in Vladivostok.

Rumbling along sedately through the forests and fields of the Russian Far East gave us a great opportunity to talk about our Russian experience and put it in some perspective within our wider journey. From the beginning we had known our traverse of Russia would be the most physically demanding part of our travels but we never considered it to be a test. We knew we could ride across with only the unavoidable drama and we had no intention of making it more difficult than it needed to be. No matter what we could achieve, even in the small world of adventure riders, there would always be someone who would go further, faster, lighter or tougher. The journey was always about us living our dream and not about getting to Vladivostok but, in the end, we would have done anything not to fail. We felt the weight of too many expectations to quit.

We were particularly thankful for the good humour of the Russians. For once on our travels we were deprived entirely of any useful language and we struggled to transliterate the Cyrillic script. The potential for us to fall into difficulties was greater than at any other time on our journey. However, the ordinary Russians we relied on to get ourselves fed and accommodated were wonderful. They greeted us with curiosity, good humour and friendship at every turn and made the impossible doable and the difficult easy. We know that our experience is different from that of others. We have met genuine and nice tourists who have complained of officious officials, corrupt cops and bureaucratic bureaucrats. Our admittedly trite response has been to point out that's their job! But at another level it raises the question about why our experience was so different. The first serious answer is that we were simply splashing about in a different pool of Russians. The folks we met had little experience with strangers and foreigners and were genuinely curious about us and the reason we were in their world. In short, without having met demanding tourists, they were prepared to take us as they found us and met our smiles, good humour and grateful thanks with their own. But we think there was much more to it than this and that the deeper reason was about Elephant and the nature our journey. We found, as we travelled, that the idea of the journey had a deep cultural significance that was probably universal. To journey far among strangers was seen as an honourable thing, worth doing for its own sake. Our arrival on Elephant underscored the challenge of our journey; its difficulties and, therefore, its specialness. We learned to tell the story of our journey quickly and efficiently and use it as a kind of currency. We used a map with graphics to show where we had come from without the need for language. We ended our explanation by saying, or indicating, 'and now we are here!' This usually elicited a broad smile. The personality of Elephant was the final element in the transaction. Elephant was so distinctive that a small fan club formed wherever we parked. People waved as we rode by and grown men asked to sit in the rider's seat to have their photo taken. People often said to us, 'that's my dream, too', and we often spent a half-hour or more answering questions and posing for photos and videos when we stopped in the street. We spent the time willingly even when we were filthy, exhausted and hot, because we understood that this was our part of the transaction. And, for their part, people were kind to us, and true to their own belief in the idea of the great journey. With these thoughts sloshing about in our heads we rolled on towards Vladivostok, looking forward to our arrival and the symbolic end of our odyssey; the end of our easterly journey; the chimera at the end of a continent.

In my imagination we rolled into Vladivostok like maharajahs, lumbering along and dispensing our largesse with our waves to interested bystanders. We rumbled down through the city to the harbour and surveyed the sea, basking in a feeling of wellbeing. Of course we photographed the moment and made pithy comments full of poignancy for the record.

As it turned out, it was nothing like that. About 50 kilometres out of Vladivostok the traffic started to thicken and slow as the day warmed to over 30 degrees with high humidity. By the time we reached the outskirts of the city we were bathed in sweat and fully occupied with navigating our way into the centre and negotiating traffic populated by some of the world's most irresponsibly stupid drivers. We struggled with navigation close to the port area where we were blocked by one way streets not shown as such on our map, and were hampered at every turn by gridlocked traffic. We roasted in our riding suits. By the time we parked in front of the ferry terminal my hubris had dissolved in a river of sweat. Rather than feeling elated we were both flat and tired.

Off the bike at last, we checked navigation for our hotel and snapped a photo and prepared to leave. As we pulled on our gear I turned in the general direction of St. Petersburg and shouted at no one in particular.

'Is that the best yer can do, ya bastards!'

No one answered. Jo frowned.

'Hmm,' she said. 'We're not on the ferry yet.'

We had an easy week in Vladivostok working out our next move, eating well and catching up with other travellers including Geoff and Alan, two Brits who would feature in further adventures just down the road. They had ridden a pair of Triumph Tigers from the UK to Vladivostok via the Baltic states and had been a day or two in front of us across Russia. They had discovered one of the real truisms of this type of travel: when travelling with others, no matter what you think your journey is about when you start it; by the end of the first month it is about the relationship.

Geoff was an ex-military man, a veteran of the Iraq war, widely travelled, self reliant and independent minded. Alan was a different type of guy. He had travelled little and this was the first real adventure he had been on. Travelling with Geoff had at first given Alan the confidence to be part of it but, with time and experience, Alan had worked out that he was an appendage to Geoff's adventure and didn't have as much control of events as he now wanted. None of this is intended to make any comment about either of them beyond the simple fact that relationships get strained on the road and these two were in the middle of finding that out when we met them. They were certainly both top blokes and great company for two itinerants desperate for English language conversation.

Of course, Jo and I had had more than 30 years of marriage to learn how to get along in close quarters. But even for us, there was a constant need to be more mindful of the other members of the team (we will give Elephant a part in this too) in every sort of situation. We found that some folk did better at it than others. For example, we had found a very cheap (unrenovated) hotel close to one of the tourist blocks that seemed to attract most of the travellers. One day we were walking out of the tourist hotel, having spent an hour in the foyer using the free WiFi, when we ran (almost literally) into three Dutch gents mounted on Honda Transalps. One was rushing about in a flat panic with a mobile stuck to his ear shouting at someone on the other end. The others sat apart, not communicating with each other or the shouter. All three were about our age. We introduced ourselves to one fellow and asked what the problem was. The accommodation booked for the group was not, it turned out, booked and there were no accommodation options left. No problem, we suggested, our hotel was a few yards away, was one quarter the price and had a better view and plenty of hot water. The Dutchman shrugged his shoulders.

'It's his problem,' he said. 'I don't want to get involved anymore.'

We then got a thumbnail sketch of the rapid breakdown of the relationships between the three travellers during their month on the road. It wasn't a pretty tale but it was one we were not surprised to hear. When we asked what they would do next, our correspondent shrugged again.

'I don't care what they do,' he said. 'Tomorrow I am heading off on my own to ride back to Holland.'

On that cheery note we wandered off in search of cabbage soup, beer and blinis.

During our first full day in Vladivostok we had found the only real bike shop there, which turned out to be the home of the Iron Tigers bike club. We were made welcome there and they offered the use of the workshop and yard to clean and service Elephant. In a stroke of good luck, we also turned up one set of tyres that could replace our stuffed Metzlers. They were Dunlop road-trail tyres but they were fine for the remainder of our journey.

It also didn't take us long in Vlad to work out that shipping a bike out of Russia was going to be hard work and that our best bet for a successful departure would be for Team Elephant to all go out together. Even the Russians thought that entrusting our bike to a shipping agent in Vlad was most likely to end in tears and this was enough to get us scurrying around looking at the options to get out of town.

The choice was Japan or Korea, both of which were serviced by ferries. Japan needed a customs permit for Elephant; Korea didn't. Decision made. We decided to catch the Dong Chun ferry from Zarubino (about 260 kilometres south of Vladivostok) to Sokcho, Republic of Korea, on Monday 21 July. Using a lot of free WiFi in the nearby tourist hotel, we organised an agent in the Korean city of Gimpo who would pack and ship Elephant home.

With a good night's sleep under our belts we started early on the run to the port. Of course it rained, and the road turned to mud, but we had found the ferry-less port by 11.30am. The lady at the gate said we were too early to buy a ticket and we should come back at 3pm, so we dripped all over a café floor for a few hours before returning. The port was still ferry-less and it was still raining. 'No ferry today,' said the lady, come back tomorrow at 10am.

After a long hard search we found the only hotel in town, hidden at the back of some crusty old apartment buildings up a dirt road that had turned into a river. I stopped at the bottom and looked up the hill at the cascades of water carving canyons in the road. Jo asked if I wanted her to dismount to make the ride up easier. I thought about the offer for a moment then said no, we had come too far to worry about that sort of thing now. As it eventuated, there was plenty of grip on the steep track. The rushing water had washed away all of the mud and left a surface of well washed road base. We scrambled up and found a building that looked a little hotel-like. Jo confirmed that this was indeed the place and negotiated some shelter. By the time we got inside we were wet through and cold and the rain continued to thunder down.

There was nowhere in the village to buy food but we did have some supplies we intended to consume on the ferry as we had been told that the food would be problematic. Our landlady lent us an electric jug for instant soup and we opened a tin of cod-liver and some biscuits. Cod liver is not high on our list of favourite foods but when you can't read the Cyrillic script on the can, you sometimes end up with interesting meals! Cod liver or not, within an hour we were warm, dry and fed, and had our wet riding gear hung to dry.

It would be nice to report that the rain stopped on our last day in Russia and so it did, but only just. We splashed down to the docks at the appointed 10am and started the process of figuring how to get ourselves and Elephant out. It was a long day that ended with me sitting on the dock at 6pm on a despondent Elephant while the Russians argued about the correct paperwork to get us onboard the boat. Eventually someone made a decision and, supervised by three Russian border police, I loaded Elephant. It was the only vehicle on the vehicle deck. In a way the last day sums up one element of our Russian experience: there were lots and lots of rules, but no one had a rule book.

At 10.30pm, the ferry slipped her mooring and it was '*da svidaniya* Russia'. The next morning we landed in Sokcho, Korea, and started to come to grips with another type of bureaucracy. The Koreans, it seemed, also had lots of rules, but here everyone had a rule book. We were quickly swallowed up by Korean Customs and in a few hours had been separated from about 600 Greenbacks, given an envelope full of paperwork, escorted to the gate and wished welcome to Korea.

With the rain thundering down we spent the first three nights in Korea in Sokcho. This gave us a chance to start to discover the essentials about this interesting country and to dry out our riding gear. We launched our culinary exploration at once at the raw fish market, with a great dinner shared with a Norwegian we had met on the ferry. Over the next few days we ate our fish in various ways, including a spicy hot pot and on a traditional barbecue. All were good! After three nights, however, we grew bored with waiting and decided to ride south in the rain. Rigged for wet-running we splashed down the coastal road to the south and set out to see Korea.

Over the next week we put up with the summer monsoon and rode around the country on a deep breath and two tanks of fuel.

It was not a very big place. In addition, 70 percent of the land was mountainous and the population of 48 million used every bit of flat or arable land for productive purposes. This has led to the interesting combination of heavily populated industrial centres distributed around largely unpopulated wilderness areas. Korea was also spotlessly clean, oppressively well organised and, to our New World eyes, extraordinarily homogeneous.

All of this, plus great food and reasonable prices, made the Republic of Korea a treat to visit... but we were not *entirely* at home. We thrive in places that are a little on the shambolic side, having always taken the view that there is opportunity in chaos. Sometimes organisation is a pain. Take the road system, for example. There was an extensive freeway system in Korea that criss-crossed the country but this was of academic interest only to us. motorbikes were not allowed on the freeways! And in case you think this was because of the blistering speeds on the super-highways, the maximum allowed was 100 km/h. That left the A roads. These were as good as the freeways in most other places and much of their length was divided dual carriageway. The speed limit on these roads was generally 60 km/h, and 80 km/h for short stretches; frustration central. Suddenly it was clear to us why the Korean Harley Davidson riders were having so much trouble in Russia. Riding on the smooth and well-ordered Korean roads would be poor preparation for the Siberian Plain.

We eventually ploughed Elephant into a river of traffic flowing north-west into the capital Seoul and found our way to the satellite city of Gimpo close to the shipping agent. We found cheap accommodation in a hotel that would best be classified as 'rent by the hour'. Jo noticed a wire basket in the elevator in which guests had left room keys and commented that this didn't seem very secure.

'I don't think they are going back to the room,' I chuckled and waited for the penny to drop.

The real giveaway, however, was that each time we came in Jo was given a new 'comfort pack' at reception. This neat plastic folder contained condoms, lubricant, some stuff called Stallion Gel (apparently designed to do wonders for male endurance), a cock ring and French tickler. Oh, and the fact that the first four pre-programmed channels on the huge flat screen TV were all soft-core porn was probably also an indicator worth noting.

Notwithstanding all this, the place was clean, secure and well run and the staff seemed pleased to have some longer-staying guests. It was also right in the business centre of Gimpo with dozens of restaurants within a few blocks. After months on the relatively bland food of Russia, we tried every type of Korean food we could find and relished the spicy change.

We also had a good base to spend some time cleaning Elephant and our clothes, repacking and preparing our gear for shipping. Australian quarantine authorities are notoriously strict in inspecting for dirt contamination on equipment entering the country and Elephant had certainly excelled at getting dirty. We negotiated 5 August as the day we would deliver Elephant to the shippers then organised our own flights back to Brisbane.

Our time in Seoul was well spent. Jo has always had trouble buying clothes in western cities as there is little stock in her size 6 or 8. In Korea, this was close to the average size and, for the first time in her life, everything she liked came in her size. Jo had often returned empty handed from a shopping expedition. In Seoul, she made five perfect-fit purchases before lunch. For my part, a new digital SLR camera intended to improve the quality of our photography on future journeys was expenditure enough.

One day, wandering in a back street in Seoul, we collided with our fellow travellers from Vladivostok, Geoff and Alan. They had also decided to catch the ferry out of Russia and then organise the shipping for the next leg of their journey from Korea. The relationship between the two had reached the stage where they were considering travelling the next leg of their journey separately. This seemed like a good idea to us and we went off to have dinner with Alan to convince him that the split was in his best interests.

We found a busy barbeque and checked the menu board outside. It showed a picture of a beef meal for three with a price. When the owner came up to convince us to eat in his restaurant, we pointed to the meal and asked him to confirm that the price shown was the price for the meal in the photo. Having got our confirmation, we found a table and ordered. All was fine until the bill arrived. It was much more than we had expected or thought fair.

The ensuing argument went on for 20 minutes getting more and more heated to the consternation of the diners until I demanded the proprietor call the police. When he demurred, I picked up the phone on the counter, handed it to him and demanded he make the call. Jo by this time had made her way across the lane and was sitting on a bench perhaps pretending not to be part of the group. The proprietor's wife sought her out and made an impassioned plea for her to intercede. Jo shrugged her shoulders in the universal sign indicating this was not her problem and the excited woman continued to rush around telling her story to any passer-by who would listen.

Alan reached for his wallet but I gave him one of those 'don't you dare' looks. He dropped his hand and, having decided that we were all committed, warmed to the argument and helped to restate our claim that we had been misled and that the tariff was unfair. The police eventually arrived and after much discussion in Korean, got an English speaking officer on the phone. It was quickly clear that the police didn't want to be involved in this dispute and I was asked if we could reach a deal.

'Sure,' I said. 'Tell the others that I will reach a compromise'.

I handed the phone back to the first officer. Once the translations were made I took out my wallet and made a show of removing all of the Korean money from it and offering it to the proprietor. It was about half the amount and what we had calculated would be a fair price. The owner stood and looked at the notes for a long time before taking the cash. I shook his reluctant hand, smiled and nodded to the police officer then we turned and walked out into the night.

As we walked up the street I suggested that I should shout a nightcap.

'But wasn't that the last of your Korean money?' asked Alan.

'Of course not,' I replied.

With all the arrangements made, our days became more relaxed and we started to talk about what it meant to us to get to the end of our journey. We had started with misgivings and uncertainty, unsure of where we wanted to go and what we wanted to achieve but knowing it was important to make the journey for its own sake. By the time we were relaxing in our Korean 'short-stay' hotel we felt we were not the same people who had ridden out of London a year before.

At that time we were worried we would not even get to Birmingham and were so uncertain about our ability we had hidden our ambitions from others. We had become tougher on our journey and we were now completely unsentimental about the problems that confronted us. We had learnt to celebrate the smallest of victories and walk away from our defeats without a second thought.

We had also confirmed the basic sameness of people everywhere and reaffirmed our kinship with the rest of humanity. Above all, we had discovered new things about our relationship after more than 30 years together. Both of us had become gentler and much less critical than we had been before the journey began. These were small changes, maybe, but good things nonetheless.

In the end it dawned on us that we would finish this journey in much the same place as we had started it. Our future was full of uncertainty and full of promise. We had no jobs to return to, little of our money remained, and we had no clear idea about what we would do next. What we now knew, however, was that the future was ours to make and we had the resources within us to make anything of it we wished.

Neither of us had much to say the day we delivered Elephant to the shippers. Not that there was much opportunity to talk about events. We still had hours of work to do before we were ready for the farewell. Eventually the paperwork, cleaning and packing was done and we were ready to load Elephant into the crate. I started the engine and manoeuvred Elephant to the ramp. Two workers stood by with ratchet straps. I gunned the front wheel up onto the crate and Elephant farted loudly and stalled in disgust. The workers stood waiting for the signal to move forward. The only sound to be heard was the faint whine of the fuel pump and the clicking of relays. I reached forward over the dash plate and switched off the ignition. With a final click of relays the panel lights went out and Elephant fell silent.

It was day 336 and Elephant's grand adventure was over.